Hope

President Ezra Taft Benson
President Gordon B. Hinckley
President Marion G. Romney
President Howard W. Hunter

Marvin J. Ashton   L. Tom Perry
James E. Faust   Neal A. Maxwell
Russell M. Nelson   M. Russell Ballard
Joseph B. Wirthlin   Dean L. Larsen
Richard G. Scott   Robert L. Backman
Paul H. Dunn   Gene R. Cook
John H. Groberg   Robert E. Wells
Derek A. Cuthbert   Jack H. Goaslind
J. Richard Clarke

Deseret Book Company
Salt Lake City, Utah

Original articles from which the chapters by
Ezra Taft Benson, Howard W. Hunter,
Marvin J. Ashton, James E. Faust, Gordon
B. Hinckley, Russell M. Nelson, Paul H.
Dunn, Robert L. Backman, Richard G.
Scott, M. Russell Ballard, Jack H. Goaslind,
Joseph B. Wirthlin, Marion G. Romney,
and Neal A. Maxwell have been adapted
© by Corporation of the President of The
Church of Jesus Christ of Latter-day Saints.
Reprinted by permission.

No part of this book may be reproduced in any
form or by any means without permission in writing
from the publisher, Deseret Book Company,
P.O. Box 30178, Salt Lake City, Utah 84130.
Deseret Book is a registered trademark of
Deseret Book Company.

First printing September 1988
Second printing March 1989

Library of Congress Cataloging-in-Publication Data

Hope / Ezra Taft Benson . . . [et al.].
    p.   cm.
    Writings by authorities of the Church of Jesus Christ of Latter-
day Saints originally published in various church magazines between
1974 and 1987.
    Includes index.
    ISBN 0-87579-173-5 : $9.95 (est.)
    1. Spiritual life—Mormon authors.   I. Benson, Ezra Taft.
BX8656.T54   1988
248.4'89332—dc19   88-22636
                                                        CIP

CONTENTS

CONTENTS

Contents

DO NOT DESPAIR

PRESIDENT EZRA TAFT BENSON

We live in an age when, as the Lord fore-
told, men's hearts are failing them, not
only physically but in spirit. (See D&C
45:26.) Many are giving up heart for the
battle of life. Suicide ranks as a major cause
of death of college students. As the showdown between
good and evil approaches with its accompanying trials and
tribulations, Satan is increasingly striving to overcome the
Saints with despair, discouragement, despondency, and
depression.

Yet, of all people, we as Latter-day Saints should be the
most optimistic and the least pessimistic. For while we know
that "peace shall be taken from the earth, and the devil
shall have power over his own dominion," we are also
assured that "the Lord shall have power over his saints, and
shall reign in their midst." (D&C 1:35-36.)

With the assurance that the Church shall remain intact
with God directing it through the troubled times ahead, it
then becomes our individual responsibility to see that each
of us remains faithful to the Church and its teachings. "He
that remaineth steadfast and is not overcome, the same
shall be saved." (JS–M 1:11.) To help us from being overcome by the devil's designs of despair, discouragement,

1

depression, and despondency, the Lord has provided at least a dozen ways that, if followed, will lift our spirits and send us on our way rejoicing.

First, repentance. In the Book of Mormon we read that "despair cometh because of iniquity." (Moroni 10:22.) "When I do good I feel good," said Abraham Lincoln, "and when I do bad I feel bad." Sin pulls a man down into despondency and despair. While a man may take some temporary pleasure in sin, the end result is unhappiness. "Wickedness never was happiness." (Alma 41:10.) Sin creates disharmony with God and is depressing to the spirit. Therefore, a man would do well to examine himself to see that he is in harmony with all of God's laws. Every law kept brings a particular blessing. Every law broken brings a particular blight. Those who are heavy-laden with despair should come unto the Lord, for His yoke is easy and His burden is light. (See Matthew 11:28-30.)

Second, prayer. Prayer in the hour of need is a great boon. From simple trials to our Gethsemanes, prayer—persistent prayer—can put us in touch with God, our greatest source of comfort and counsel. "Pray always, that you may come off conqueror." (D&C 10:5.) "Exerting all my powers to call upon God to deliver me" is how the young Joseph Smith describes the method that he used in the Sacred Grove to keep the adversary from destroying him. (JS–H 1:16.) This is also a key to use in keeping depression from destroying us.

Third, service. To lose yourself in righteous service to others can lift your sights and get your mind off personal problems, or at least put them in proper focus. "When you find yourselves a little gloomy," said President Lorenzo Snow, "look around you and find somebody that is in a worse plight than yourself; go to him and find out what the trouble is, then try to remove it with the wisdom which

2

the Lord bestows upon you; and the first thing you know, your gloom is gone, you feel light, the Spirit of the Lord is upon you, and everything seems illuminated." (Conference Report, 6 April 1899, pp. 2-3.)

A woman whose life is involved in the righteous rearing of her children has a better chance of keeping up her spirits than the woman whose total concern is centered in her own personal problems.

Fourth, work. The earth was cursed for Adam's sake. Work is our blessing, not our doom. God has a work to do, and so should we. Retirement from work has depressed many a man and hastened his death. It has been said that even the very fiends weave ropes of sand rather than face the pure hell of idleness. We should work at taking care of the spiritual, mental, social, and physical needs of ourselves and of those whom we are charged to help. In the church of Jesus Christ, there is plenty of work to do to move forward the kingdom of God. Missionary work, family genealogy and temple work, home evenings, receiving a Church assignment and magnifying it are but a few of our required labors.

Fifth, health. The condition of the physical body can affect the spirit. That's why the Lord gave us the Word of Wisdom. He also said that we should retire to our beds early and arise early (see D&C 88:124), that we should not run faster than we have strength (see D&C 10:4), and that we should use moderation in all good things. In general, the more food we eat in its natural state—without additives— and the less it is refined, the healthier it will be for us. Food can affect the mind, and deficiencies of certain elements in the body can promote mental depression. A good physical examination periodically is a safeguard and may spot problems that can be remedied. Rest and physical exercise are essential, and a walk in the fresh air can refresh the spirit.

Wholesome recreation is part of our religion and is a necessary change of pace; even its anticipation can lift the spirit.

Sixth, reading. Many a man in his hour of trial has turned to the Book of Mormon and been enlightened, enlivened, and comforted.

The psalms in the Old Testament have a special food for the soul of one in distress. In our day, we are additionally blessed with the Doctrine and Covenants—modern revelation. The words of the prophets are crucial reading and can give direction and comfort in an hour when one is down.

Seventh, receiving a blessing. In a particularly stressful time, or in the anticipation of a critical event, one can seek for a blessing under the hands of the priesthood. Even the Prophet Joseph Smith sought and received a blessing under the hands of Brigham Young and received solace and direction for his soul. Fathers, so live that you can bless your own wives and children. To receive and then consistently and prayerfully ponder one's patriarchal blessing can give helpful insight, particularly in an hour of need. The sacrament will "bless . . . the souls" (D&C 20:77, 79) of all those who worthily partake of it, and as such it should be taken often, even by the bedfast, who can arrange with their bishop to receive the sacrament at home or at the hospital.

Eighth, fasting. A certain kind of devil goes not out except by fasting and prayer, the scriptures tell us. (See Matthew 17:14-21.) Periodic fasting can help clear up the mind and strengthen the body and the spirit. The usual fast, the one we are asked to participate in for fast Sunday, is to abstain from food and drink for two consecutive meals. Some people, feeling the need, have gone on longer fasts of abstaining from food but have taken the needed liquids.

Wisdom should be used, and this fast should be broken with light eating. To make a fast more fruitful, it should be coupled with prayer and meditation; physical work should be held to a minimum, and one should ponder on the scriptures and the reason for the fast.

Ninth, friends. The fellowship of true friends who can hear you out, share your joys, help carry your burdens, and correctly counsel you is priceless. For one who has been in the prison of depression, the words of the Prophet Joseph Smith have special meaning: "How sweet the voice of a friend is; one token of friendship from any source whatever awakens and calls into action every sympathetic feeling." (*Teachings of the Prophet Joseph Smith,* comp. Joseph Fielding Smith, Salt Lake City: Deseret Book Co., 1938, p. 134.)

Ideally, our family ought to be our closest friends. Most important, we should seek to become the friend of our Father in Heaven and our brother Jesus the Christ. What a boon to be in the company of those who edify us! To have friends, one should be friendly. Friendship should begin at home and then be extended to encompass the home teacher, quorum leader, bishop, and other Church teachers and leaders. To meet often with the Saints and enjoy their companionship can buoy up the heart.

Tenth, music. Inspiring music may fill the soul with heavenly thoughts, move one to righteous action, or speak peace to the soul. When Saul was troubled with an evil spirit, David played for him with his harp; Saul was refreshed and the evil spirit departed. (See 1 Samuel 16:23.) Elder Boyd K. Packer has wisely suggested memorizing some of the inspiring songs of Zion and then, when the mind is afflicted with temptations, singing aloud, to keep before your mind the inspiring words and crowd out the evil thoughts. (See *Ensign,* January 1974, p. 28.) This could also be done to crowd out debilitating, depressing thoughts.

Eleventh, endurance. When George A. Smith was very ill, he was visited by his cousin, the Prophet Joseph Smith. The afflicted man reported: "He [the Prophet] told me I should never get discouraged, whatever difficulties might surround me. If I were sunk into the lowest pit of Nova Scotia and all the Rocky Mountains piled on top of me, I ought not to be discouraged, but hang on, exercise faith, and keep up good courage, and I should come out on the top of the heap." (*George A. Smith Family,* comp. Zora Smith Jarvis, Provo, Utah: Brigham Young University Press, 1962, p. 54.)

There are times when you simply have to righteously hang on and outlast the devil until his depressive spirit leaves you. As the Lord told the Prophet Joseph Smith: "Thine adversity and thine afflictions shall be but a small moment;

"And then, if thou endure it well, God shall exalt thee on high." (D&C 121:7-8.)

Pressing on in noble endeavors, even while surrounded by a cloud of depression, will eventually bring you out on top into the sunshine. Even our master Jesus the Christ, while facing that supreme test of being temporarily left alone by our Father during the Crucifixion, continued performing His labors for the children of men, and then shortly thereafter He was glorified and received a fulness of joy. While you are going through your trial, you can recall your past victories and count the blessings that you do have with a sure hope of greater ones to follow if you are faithful. And you can have that certain knowledge that in due time God will wipe away all tears and that "eye hath not seen, nor ear heard, neither have entered into the heart of man, the things which God hath prepared for them that love him." (1 Corinthians 2:9.)

Twelfth, goals. Every accountable child of God needs

to set goals, short- and long-range goals. A man who is pressing forward to accomplish worthy goals can soon put despondency under his feet, and once a goal is accomplished, others can be set up. Some will be continuing goals. Each week when we partake of the sacrament we commit ourselves to the goals of taking upon ourselves the name of Christ, of always remembering Him and keeping His commandments. Of Jesus' preparations for His mission, the scripture states that He "increased in wisdom and stature, and in favour with God and man." (Luke 2:52.) This encompasses four main areas for goals: spiritual, mental, physical, and social. "Therefore, what manner of men ought ye to be?" asked the Master, and He answered, "Verily I say unto you, even as I am." (3 Nephi 27:27.) Now, there is a lifetime goal—to walk in His steps, to perfect ourselves in every virtue as He has done, to seek His face, and to work to make our calling and election sure.

"Brethren," said Paul, "but this one thing I do, forgetting those things which are behind, and reaching forth unto those things which are before,

"I press toward the mark for the prize of the high calling of God in Christ Jesus." (Philippians 3:13-14.)

Let your minds be filled with the goal of being like the Lord, and you will crowd out depressing thoughts as you anxiously seek to know Him and do His will. "Let this mind be in you," said Paul. (Philippians 2:5.) "Look unto me in every thought," said Jesus. (D&C 6:36.) And what will follow if we do? "Thou wilt keep him in perfect peace, whose mind is stayed on thee." (Isaiah 26:3.)

"Salvation," said the Prophet Joseph Smith, "is nothing more nor less than to triumph over all our enemies and put them under our feet." (*Teachings*, p. 297.) We can rise above the enemies of despair, depression, discouragement, and despondency by remembering that God provides righteous alternatives, some of which I have mentioned. As it states in the Bible, "There hath no temptation taken you but such as is common to man: but God is faithful, who will not suffer you to be tempted above that ye are able; but will with the temptation also make a way to escape, that ye may be able to bear it." (1 Corinthians 10:13.)

Yes, life is a test; it is a probation; and perhaps being away from our heavenly home we feel sometimes, as holy men in the past have felt, that we are "strangers and pilgrims on the earth." (See D&C 45:13.)

Some of you will recall in that great book *Pilgrim's Progress* by John Bunyan that the main character known as Christian was trying to press forward to gain entrance to the celestial city. He made it to his goal, but in order to do so, he had to overcome many obstacles, one of which was to escape from the Giant Despair. To lift our spirits and send us on our way rejoicing, the devil's designs of despair, discouragement, depression, and despondency can be defeated in a dozen ways, namely: repentance, prayer, service, work, health, reading, blessings, fasting, friends, music, endurance, and goals.

May we use them all in the difficult days ahead so that we Christian pilgrims will have greater happiness here and go on to a fulness of joy in the highest realms of the celestial kingdom.

THE OPENING AND CLOSING OF DOORS

PRESIDENT HOWARD W. HUNTER

I have observed that life — every life — has a full share of ups and downs. Indeed, we see many joys and sorrows in the world, many changed plans and new directions, many blessings that do not always feel like blessings, and much that humbles us and improves our patience and our faith. We have all had those experiences from time to time, and I suppose we always will.

A passage from one of the greatest prophetic sermons ever given — King Benjamin's masterful discourse to the people of Zarahemla in the Book of Mormon — reads this way:

"Men drink damnation to their own souls except they humble themselves and become as little children. . . .

"For the natural man is an enemy to God, and has been from the fall of Adam, and will be, forever and ever, unless he yields to the enticings of the Holy Spirit, and putteth off the natural man and becometh a saint through the atonement of Christ the Lord, and becometh as a child, submissive, meek, humble, patient, full of love, willing to submit to all things which the Lord seeth fit to inflict upon him, even as a child doth submit to his father." (Mosiah 3:18-19.)

Being childlike and submitting to our Father's will is

9

not always easy. President Spencer W. Kimball, who knew a good deal about suffering, disappointment, and circumstances beyond his control, once wrote:

"Being human, we would expel from our lives physical pain and mental anguish and assure ourselves of continual ease and comfort, but if we were to close the doors upon sorrow and distress, we might be excluding our greatest friends and benefactors. Suffering can make saints of people as they learn patience, long-suffering, and self-mastery." (*Faith Precedes the Miracle,* Salt Lake City: Deseret Book Co., 1972, p. 98.)

In that statement, President Kimball refers to closing doors upon certain experiences in life. That image brings to mind a line from Cervantes' great classic, *Don Quixote,* that has given me comfort over the years. In that masterpiece, we find the short but very important reminder that where one door closes, another opens. Doors close regularly in our lives, and some of those closings cause genuine pain and heartache. But I *do* believe that where one such door closes, another opens (and perhaps more than one), with hope and blessings in other areas of our lives that we might not have discovered otherwise.

President Marion G. Romney had some doors swing closed for him even in the work of his ministry. He knew considerable pain and discouragement and saw his plans change during the last few years of his life. But it was he who said that all men and women, including the most faithful and loyal, would find adversity and affliction in their lives because, in the words of Joseph Smith, "Men have to suffer that they may come upon Mount Zion and be exalted above the heavens." (*History of the Church of Jesus Christ of Latter-day Saints,* 7 vols., ed. B.H. Roberts, Salt Lake City: The Church of Jesus Christ of Latter-day Saints, 1932-51, 5:556; see Conference Report, October 1969, p. 57.)

President Romney then said: "This does not mean that we crave suffering. We avoid all we can. However, we now know, and we all knew when we elected to come into mortality, that we would here be proved in the crucible of adversity and affliction. . . .

"[Furthermore,] the Father's plan for proving [and refining] his children did not exempt the Savior himself. The suffering he undertook to endure, and which he did endure, equaled the combined suffering of all men [and women] everywhere. Trembling and bleeding and wishing to shrink from the cup, he said, 'I partook and finished my preparations unto the children of men.' (D&C 19:18-19.)" (Conference Report, October 1969, p. 57.)

All of us must finish our "preparations unto the children of men." Christ's preparations were quite different from our own, but we all have preparations to make, doors to open. To make such important preparations often will require some pain, some unexpected changes in life's path, and some submitting, "even as a child doth submit to his father." Finishing divine preparations and opening celestial doors may take us—indeed, undoubtedly will take us—right up to the concluding hours of our mortal lives.

We all miss our beloved brother Elder A. Theodore Tuttle, who has opened a new door to return to his heavenly home. His preparations in mortality had been fully completed for such a journey. He, too, like President Romney, spoke of adversity, adversity that he knew would come to each of us but that he may not then have known would come to him as early as it did.

He said: "Adversity, in one form or another, is the universal experience of man. It is the common lot of all . . . to experience misfortune, suffering, sickness, or other adversities. Ofttimes our work is arduous and unnecessarily demanding. Our faith is tried in various ways—sometimes unjustly tried [it seems]. At times it seems that even God is punishing us and ours. One of the things that makes all this so hard to bear is that we ourselves appear to be chosen for this affliction while others presumably escape these adversities. . . . [But] we cannot indulge ourselves the luxury of self-pity." (Conference Report, October 1967, pp. 14-15.)

Elder Tuttle then quoted these lines from Robert Browning Hamilton titled "Along the Road," which teach a lesson on pleasure and a lesson on sorrow:

> I walked a mile with Pleasure;
> She chattered all the way,
> But left me none the wiser
> For all she had to say.
> I walked a mile with Sorrow,
> And ne'er a word said she;
> But oh, the things I learned from her
> When Sorrow walked with me!

And now this mortal portion of Elder Tuttle's journey is over. He closed that door and opened another. Now he walks and talks with the angels. And so, someday, will we close and open those same doors.

I have mentioned the lives of two of our contemporary Brethren. Obviously, prophets of an earlier day have known adversity and difficulty as well. They were not spared these challenges any more than our generation has been spared. The great Book of Mormon patriarch, Lehi, spoke encouragingly to his son Jacob, a son born in the wilderness in a time of travail and opposition. Jacob's life was not as he might have expected it to be and not as the ideal course of experience might have outlined. He had suffered afflictions and setbacks, but Lehi promised that such afflictions would be consecrated for his son's gain. (See 2 Nephi 2:2.)

12

Then Lehi added these words that have become classic: "For it must needs be, that there is an opposition in all things. If not so, . . . righteousness could not be brought to pass, neither wickedness, neither holiness nor misery, neither good nor bad." (2 Nephi 2:11.)

I have taken great comfort over the years in this explanation of some of life's pain and disappointment. I take even greater comfort that the greatest of men and women, including the Son of God, have faced such opposition in order to better understand the contrast between righteousness and wickedness, holiness and misery, good and bad. From out of the dark, damp confinement of Liberty Jail, the Prophet Joseph Smith learned that if we are called to pass through tribulation, it is for our growth and experience and will ultimately be counted for our good. (See D&C 122:5-8.)

Where one door shuts, another opens, even for a prophet in prison. We are not always wise enough or experienced enough to judge adequately all of the possible entries and exits. The mansion that God prepares for each of His beloved children may have only certain hallways and banisters, special carpets and curtains that He would have us pass on our way to possess it.

I share the view expressed by Orson F. Whitney in these words: "No pain that we suffer, no trial that we experience is wasted. It ministers to our education, to the development of such qualities as patience, faith, fortitude, and humility. All that we suffer and all that we endure, especially when we endure it patiently, builds up our characters, purifies our hearts, expands our souls, and makes us more tender and charitable, more worthy to be called the children of God . . . and it is through sorrow and suffering, toil and tribulation, that we gain the education that we come here to acquire and which will make us more like our Father and

Mother in heaven." (As quoted in *Faith Precedes the Miracle*, p. 98.)

At various times in our lives, probably at repeated times in our lives, we do have to acknowledge that God knows what we do not know and sees what we do not see. "For my thoughts are not your thoughts, neither are your ways my ways, saith the Lord." (Isaiah 55:8.)

If you have troubles at home with children who stray, if you suffer financial reverses and emotional strain that threaten your homes and your happiness, if you must face the loss of life or health, may peace be unto your soul. We will not be tempted beyond our ability to withstand. Our detours and disappointments are the straight and narrow path to Him, as we sing in one of our favorite hymns:

> When through fiery trials thy pathway shall lie,
> My grace, all sufficient, shall be thy supply.
> The flame shall not hurt thee; I only design
> Thy dross to consume and thy gold to refine.
> ("How Firm a Foundation," *Hymns*, Salt Lake City: The Church of Jesus Christ of Latter-day Saints, 1985, no. 85.)

May God bless us in the ups and downs of life, in the opening and closing of doors.

ADVERSITY AND YOU

ELDER MARVIN J. ASHTON

I remember an occasion when I listened to two of my
friends discuss their favorite football team. They were
in agreement that possibly the greatest limiting factor
in the team's achieving high national ranking was its
game schedule. They felt the team, for its own good,
should play against stronger competition.

In football or in life, the adversaries, the ones with
whom we compete, the ones we oppose or resist—our op-
ponents, our foes, our enemies, or our problems—are often
the determining factors in our ultimate strength and
achievement.

Adversity will surface in some form in every life. How
we prepare for it, how we meet it, makes the difference.
We can be broken by adversity, or we can become stronger.
The final result is up to the individual. Henry Fielding said:
"Adversity is the trial of principle. Without it, a man hardly
knows whether he is honest or not." (In *The New Dictionary
of Thoughts*, ed. Ralph Emerson Browns, n.p.: Standard
Book Co., 1957, p. 6.)

Realizing that adversity can include suffering, destitu-
tion, affliction, calamity, or disaster, how can we best use it
as an opportunity for personal growth and development?
For one answer, let me share with you an incident in the

life of a special friend, which he tells in his own words at my request. I find his experience a powerful sermon.

"It was the third Saturday in January a few years ago. I was excited to attend a seminar that morning. It was an agricultural seminar at Brigham Young University, where I had been attending school. I had been home from my Honolulu Hawaii Mission six months and was going through all the adjustments of a returned missionary. The challenge of family, girls, school, and the fact that there were twenty-five thousand other students who were bright and aggressive—some with plenty of money; others, like myself, who were pinching every nickel—didn't make things easier.

"I landed a job running a hydraulic press earlier that week in a machine shop. We made seals for hydraulic equipment. Following the seminar that morning, I went to work. Kimball, my roommate and former missionary companion who had gone to work earlier that morning, instructed me in how to make a new seal. After approximately twenty minutes, one of the smallest seals stuck on the face of the plate. I struggled to get it off with my left hand. As I turned back to give it my full attention and use my right hand, the machine closed on my left hand, causing a horrible noise as it crushed my hand just below the wrist. After what seemed an eternity, the huge press finally opened. My first thought when looking at my hand was 'What a mess!' Then that inner voice which I had come to know, love, and appreciate, whispered, 'Jerry, you won't have your hand.'

"Four hours of surgery followed. The first thing I remember hearing was the surgeon's voice in the recovery room.

" 'Jerry,' he said, 'Can you hear me?'

" 'Yes,' I said.

" 'We had to take your hand off.'

"The following four days were filled with tears, aches,

friends, cards, letters, and family. Concerned people made it so much easier for me, especially Kimball. He let my parents and others close to me know and helped in every way he could. Never did I have to ask for one thing. It was already done. By his example and support, he gave me courage to face this new challenge.

"The days in the hospital were filled with painful, sleepless hours and nights. Those nights gave me an opportunity to think about the Savior and Joseph Smith as I had never done before. I reviewed the Prophet Joseph's life from everything I had learned. He faced physical, emotional, and spiritual trial upon trial. How I marveled at his well-won victories! At this difficult time I promised the Lord I would try to accept all of my challenges as the Prophet Joseph Smith had accepted his.

"Of course, during the first night there were thoughts of 'Why me? Was it something in my past? What have I done to deserve this?' Then I thought, 'No more rodeo, football, or skiing,' and I wondered what type of a woman would want a one-handed husband. I hadn't developed a good self-image or a great deal of self-esteem, so these thoughts magnified my concerns.

"Mom came to school and drove me home for the weekend. One thing she said that made me again appreciate her greatness was, 'Jerry, if I could only give you my left hand and make it work, I would.'

"Sunday was fast Sunday. As I stood favoring my bandaged, shortened arm, I thanked everyone for their thoughts, prayers, and cards. I realized as never before that good friends and faithful family members make challenges less difficult.

"After the testimony meeting, an admired friend gave me a special blessing. So many questions were answered during his blessing. He told me this accident was not punishment for anything I had done but, rather, an opportunity to help me become a better person and to amplify those particular traits which needed to be developed. He shared the thought that this challenge could make me more understanding of people, problems, and life. As I look back now, each point of his blessing and encouragement has helped in a very fulfilling way.

"One of my greatest fears was the constant thought of how people would accept me. Would they be afraid of me, question my ability, or write me off before I could prove myself? Would girls turn down dates because I was different? Would it make them feel uncomfortable to be seen with me?

"I had dated several girls since my mission but had only dated Julie a couple of times. When I awoke the day following the operation in the hospital, she was there with other friends. I asked everyone else to leave the room, and I then proceeded to give her what I thought was the perfect speech. I told her that they had to take my hand off. If she felt embarrassed or ashamed to be with me or be seen with me on future dates, she need not feel obligated to continue in any future courtship. At that moment I could see fire in her eyes. She let me know in no uncertain terms that she was not there out of pity or duty, but only because she cared for me. She indicated she would help me but never feel sorry for me. Six months later we were married in the Salt Lake Temple.

"There were many job interviews, prejudices, and rejections of employment; but with continued encouragement, the Lord blessed us in innumerable ways. When our first little girl, Bracken, arrived, it left us short of money to go to school. So after a major decision, we went into business, which proved to be another learning experience. After a couple of years—with many reverses—I was able to find a career in personnel management, which not only fulfilled my goals but also answered my prayers.

"Today as I look back, I see the challenge of adversity as something upon which to build. Of course, I cannot say the experience was pleasant; it was horrible. However, I hope I have used this adversity in a positive way. When I see others in trouble, in pain, when real adversity is knocking, I have an opportunity not only to feel something of what they feel, but perhaps I can also help them because they can see that I have challenges of my own."

Following a recent discussion on the subject of adversity, a young man who was greatly concerned about the burdens being carried by his wonderful mother asked the question, "If God is omnipotent and knows all, why does He put my mother through the agony of continual sufferings when He already knows what the outcome will be?" Our response was, "Your mother's trials are not tests so the Lord can measure her. They are tests and trials so that your mother can measure herself. It is most important that she know her strengths in adversity and grow from the experiences."

When, with several companions, the Prophet Joseph Smith was a prisoner in Liberty, Missouri, for a number of months, conditions were deplorable. Their petitions and appeals directed to executive officers and the judiciary had failed to bring relief. In desperation Joseph pleaded for understanding and assistance from his Heavenly Father. The message finally came:

"My son, peace be unto thy soul; thine adversity and thine afflictions shall be but a small moment;

"And then, if thou endure it well, God shall exalt thee on high; thou shalt triumph over all thy foes." (D&C 121:7-8.)

It can be declared accurately and without hesitation that Joseph Smith's noble character and stature were shaped and achieved by constant victories over his afflictions. Jesus, too, developed unique balance mentally, physically, spiritually, and socially as He labored and served under all types of trying circumstances:

"Though he were a Son, yet learned he obedience by the things which he suffered;

"And being made perfect, he became the author of eternal salvation unto all them that obey him." (Hebrews 5:8-9.)

Difficulties can be a valuable tool in our pursuit for perfection. Adversity need have no necessary connection with failure. Proper self-management and self-discipline in all of our trials bring strength. If we are prepared, we can meet life's challenges victoriously. We become His disciples when we continue faithfully under all circumstances—including suffering and tragedy.

C. S. Lewis shared a meaningful observation when he said, "I have seen great beauty of spirit in some who were great sufferers. I have seen men, for the most part, grow better not worse with advancing years, and I have seen the last illness produce treasures of fortitude and meekness from most unpromising subjects."

I have another choice friend who has known very few days in his life which were not filled with pain, discomfort, or disease. He shakes his fists at the forces of darkness and trial. His taxing trials of all of the yesterdays have been properly met and have assisted in making him what he is today. Like Caleb of old, he too can be heard to say, "As yet I am . . . strong. . . . Now therefore give me this mountain." (Joshua 14:11, 12). More mountains, even those high in adversity, can better prepare us for tomorrow if we are but willing to climb.

Jesus Christ, the Master, shares His life of trials and victories with us for our motivation and direction. God strengthened His Son. He, too, will support us, His children, if we will turn to Him for guidance.

What a blessing it is to know that we can be supported against all the fiery darts of the enemy if we are faithful. A worthy daily prayer is one asking for the power to be faithful under all circumstances.

Knowing that Satan and his hosts are relentless in their attempts to ridicule, embarrass, belittle, and cause all of us to yield and ultimately fall, what should be our attitude in today's society? There is an important step beyond avoiding contention and strife; and that is to live with dignity. There is something sacred about living with dignity. We need not quarrel or compete with those who promote and encourage controversy. We need not spend our time in retaliation. They who would deceive, destroy, or belittle reap their own rewards. Their works are neither praiseworthy nor of good report. How disarming it must be to the enemies to see the valiant moving forward with poise and dignity under all challenging circumstances. Scorn and ridicule are two of the greatest forms of adversity we are required to face in today's world. Doing the will of God on a daily basis leaves no time for contention or confrontation.

From Harry Emerson Fosdick we read, "The most extraordinary thing about the oyster is this. Irritations get into his shell. He does not like them. But when he cannot get rid of them, he uses the irritation to do the loveliest thing an oyster ever has a chance to do. If there are irritations in our lives today, there is only one prescription: make a pearl. It may have to be a pearl of patience, but, anyhow, make a pearl. And it takes faith and love to do it." (In *The Treasure Chest*, ed. Charles L. Wallis, New York: Harper & Row.)

Those who yield to adversity become weaker. To the valiant it is a stepping-stone to increased power. Members of The Church of Jesus Christ of Latter-day Saints and God-fearing people worldwide will not pray for freedom from trials. They will not surrender or panic. They will strive to put themselves in condition to meet and master troublesome trials.

Usually there are no easy answers to most of our problems. Each individual must think, plan, work, and pray to find the help he needs and the courage he must have to conquer his problem or carry his cross—whatever his lot may be. Winners set achievable goals day by day. Their plans consist of things that can be done, not what can't be done. They remember that God has not given us the spirit of fear, but the power of love and of a sound mind.

God seems to have sustaining love for those like Jerry who are coping courageously with adversity. In many cases it seems they have a special relationship with Him. "Behold, I have refined thee. . . . I have chosen thee in the furnace of affliction." (Isaiah 48:10.)

Individually, we should thank God for the examples of those about us who battle and conquer daily challenges that are intense, real, and continuing. There are some persons who in our human eyes seem to have more than their share of trouble, as we measure, but with God's help they are made special. They will not break. They will not yield.

Satan wants us to feel unequal to our worldly tasks. If we turn to God, He will take us by the hand and lead us through our darkest hours.

THE REFINER'S FIRE

ELDER JAMES E. FAUST

I direct my thoughts to all, but especially to those who feel they have had more trials, sorrows, pricks, and thorns than they can bear and in their adversity are almost drowned in the waters of bitterness. My message is intended as one of hope, strength, and deliverance. I speak of the refiner's fire.

Some years ago President David O. McKay told of the experience of some of those in the Martin handcart company. Many of these early converts had emigrated from Europe and were too poor to buy oxen or horses and a wagon. They were forced by their poverty to pull handcarts containing all of their belongings across the plains by their own brute strength. President McKay relates an occurrence which took place some years after the heroic exodus: "A teacher, conducting a class, said it was unwise ever to attempt, even to permit [the Martin handcart company] to come across the plains under such conditions.

"[According to a class member] some sharp criticism of the Church and its leaders was being indulged in for permitting any company of converts to venture across the plains with no more supplies or protection than a handcart caravan afforded.

"An old man in the corner . . . sat silent and listened

23

as long as he could stand it, then he arose and said things that no person who heard him will ever forget. His face was white with emotion, yet he spoke calmly, deliberately, but with great earnestness and sincerity.

"In substance [he] said, 'I ask you to stop this criticism. You are discussing a matter you know nothing about. Cold historic facts mean nothing here, for they give no proper interpretation of the questions involved. Mistake to send the Handcart Company out so late in the season? Yes. But I was in that company and my wife was in it and Sister Nellie Unthank whom you have cited was there, too. We suffered beyond anything you can imagine and many died of exposure and starvation, but did you ever hear a survivor of that company utter a word of criticism? *Not one of that company ever apostatized or left the Church, because everyone of us came through with the absolute knowledge that God lives, for we became acquainted with him in our extremities.*

" 'I have pulled my handcart when I was so weak and weary from illness and lack of food that I could hardly put one foot ahead of the other. I have looked ahead and seen a patch of sand or a hill slope and I have said, I can go only that far and there I must give up, for I cannot pull the load through it.' "

He continues: " 'I have gone on to that sand and when I reached it, the cart began pushing me. I have looked back many times to see who was pushing my cart, but my eyes saw no one. I knew then that the angels of God were there.

" 'Was I sorry that I chose to come by handcart? No. Neither then nor any minute of my life since. The price we paid to become acquainted with God was a privilege to pay, and I am thankful that I was privileged to come in the Martin Handcart Company.' " (*Relief Society Magazine*, January 1948, p. 8.)

Here, then, is a great truth. In the pain, the agony,

and the heroic endeavors of life, we pass through a refiner's fire, and the insignificant and the unimportant in our lives can melt away like dross and make our faith bright, intact, and strong. In this way the divine image can be mirrored from the soul. It is part of the purging toll exacted of some to become acquainted with God. In the agonies of life, we seem to listen better to the faint, godly whisperings of the Divine Shepherd.

Into every life there come the painful, despairing days of adversity and buffeting. There seems to be a full measure of anguish, sorrow, and often heartbreak for everyone, including those who earnestly seek to do right and be faithful. The thorns that prick, that stick in the flesh, that hurt, often change lives that seem robbed of significance and hope. This change comes about through a refining process that often seems cruel and hard. In this way the soul can become like soft clay in the hands of the Master in building lives of faith, usefulness, beauty, and strength. For some, the refiner's fire causes a loss of belief and faith in God, but those with eternal perspective understand that such refining is part of the perfection process.

In our extremities, it is possible to become born again, born anew, renewed in heart and spirit. We no longer ride with the flow of the crowd, but instead we enjoy the promise of Isaiah to be renewed in our strength and "mount up with wings as eagles." (Isaiah 40:31.)

The proving of one's faith goes before the witnessing, for Moroni testified, "Ye receive no witness until after the trial of your faith." (Ether 12:6.) This trial of faith can become a priceless experience. Stated Peter, "That the trial of your faith, being much more precious than of gold that perisheth, though it be tried with fire, might be found unto praise and honour and glory at the appearing of Jesus

Christ." (1 Peter 1:7.) Trials and adversity can be preparatory to becoming born anew.

A rebirth out of spiritual adversity causes us to become new creatures. From the book of Mosiah we learn that all mankind must be born again—born of God, changed, redeemed, and uplifted—to become the sons and daughters of God. (See Mosiah 27:24-27.)

President Marion G. Romney, speaking for the Lord, has said of this marvelous power: "The effect upon each person's life is likewise similar. No person whose soul is illuminated by the burning Spirit of God can in this world of sin and dense darkness remain passive. He is driven by an irresistible urge to fit himself to be an active agent of God in furthering righteousness and in freeing the lives and minds of men from the bondage of sin." (Conference Report, 4 October 1941, p. 89.)

The feelings of being reborn were expressed by Parley P. Pratt as follows: "If I had been set to turn the world over, to dig down a mountain, to go to the ends of the earth, or traverse the deserts of Arabia, it would have been easier than to have undertaken to rest, while the Priesthood was upon me. I have received the holy anointing, and I can never rest till the last enemy is conquered, death destroyed, and truth reigns triumphant." (Journal of Discourses, 26 vols., London: Latter-day Saints' Book Depot, 1854-86, 1:15.)

Unfortunately, some of our greatest tribulations are the result of our own foolishness and weakness and occur because of our own carelessness or transgression. Central to solving these problems is the great need to get back on the right track and, if necessary, engage in each of the steps for full and complete repentance. Through this great principle, many things can be made fully right and all things better. We can go to others for help. To whom can we go? Elder

Orson F. Whitney asked and answered this question: "To whom do we look, in days of grief and disaster, for help and consolation? . . . They are men and women who have suffered, and out of their experience in suffering they bring forth the riches of their sympathy and condolences as a blessing to those now in need. Could they do this had they not suffered themselves?

" . . . Is not this God's purpose in causing his children to suffer? He wants them to become more like himself. God has suffered far more than man ever did or ever will, and is therefore the great source of sympathy and consolation." (*Improvement Era,* November 1918, p. 7.)

Isaiah, before the Savior's birth, referred to Him as "a man of sorrows." (Isaiah 53:3.) Speaking in the Doctrine and Covenants of Himself, the Savior said: "Which suffering caused myself, even God, the greatest of all, to tremble because of pain, and to bleed at every pore, and to suffer both body and spirit—and would that I might not drink the bitter cup, and shrink." (D&C 19:18.)

Some are prone to feel that their afflictions are punishment. Roy Doxey states: "The Prophet Joseph Smith taught that it is a false idea to believe that the saints will escape all the judgments—disease, pestilence, war, etc.—of the last days; consequently, it is an unhallowed principle to say that these adversities are due to transgression. . . .

"President Joseph F. Smith taught that it is a feeble thought to believe that the illness and affliction that come to us are attributable either to the mercy or the displeasure of God." (*The Doctrine and Covenants Speaks,* Salt Lake City: Deseret Book Co., 1970, 2:373.)

Paul understood this perfectly. When referring to the Savior, he said: "Though he were a Son, yet learned he obedience by the things which he suffered;

"And being made perfect, he became the author of

27

eternal salvation unto all them that obey him." (Hebrews 5:8-9.)

For some, the suffering is extraordinary.

Stillman Pond was a member of the second Quorum of Seventy in Nauvoo. He was an early convert to the Church, having come from Hubbardston, Massachusetts. Like others, he and his wife, Maria, and their children were harassed and driven out of Nauvoo. In September 1846, they became part of the great western migration. The early winter that year brought extreme hardships, including malaria, cholera, and consumption. The family was visited by all three of these diseases.

Maria contracted consumption and all of the children were stricken with malaria. Three of the children died while moving through the early snows. Stillman buried them on the plains. Maria's condition worsened because of the grief, pain, and the fever of malaria. She could no longer walk. Weakened and sickly, she gave birth to twins. They were named Joseph and Hyrum, and both died within a few days.

The Stillman Pond family arrived at Winter Quarters and, like many other families, they suffered bitterly while living in a tent. The death of the five children coming across the plains to Winter Quarters was but a beginning.

The journal of Horace K. and Helen Mar Whitney verifies the following regarding four more of the children of Stillman Pond who perished:

"On Wednesday, the 2nd of December 1846, Laura Jane Pond, age 14 years, . . . died of chills and fever." Two days later on "Friday, the 4th of December 1846, Harriet M. Pond, age 11 years, . . . died with chills." Three days later, "Monday, the 7th of December, 1846, Abigail A. Pond, age 18 years, . . . died with chills." Just five weeks later, "Friday, the 15th of January, 1847, Lyman Pond, age 6 years, . . . died with chills and fever." Four months later, on May 17, 1847, his wife Maria Davis Pond also died. Crossing the plains, Stillman Pond lost nine children and a wife. He became an outstanding colonizer in Utah, and became the senior president of the thirty-fifth Quorum of Seventy. (See Leon Y. and H. Ray Pond, comps., "Stillman Pond, a Biographical Sketch," in *Sterling Forsyth Histories,* typescript, Church Historical Department Archives, pp. 4-5.)

Having lost these nine children and his wife in crossing the plains, Stillman Pond did not lose his faith. He did not quit. He went forward. He paid a price, as have many others before and since, to become acquainted with God.

The Divine Shepherd has a message of hope, strength, and deliverance for all. If there were no night, we would not appreciate the day, nor could we see the stars and the vastness of the heavens. We must partake of the bitter with the sweet. There is a divine purpose in the adversities we encounter every day. They prepare, they purge, they purify, and thus they bless.

When we pluck the roses, we find we often cannot avoid the thorns which spring from the same stem.

Out of the refiner's fire can come a glorious deliverance. It can be a noble and lasting rebirth. The price to become acquainted with God will have been paid. There will be a reawakening of dormant, inner resources. A comfortable cloak of righteousness will be drawn around us to protect us and to keep us warm spiritually. Self-pity will vanish as our blessings are counted.

I now wish to conclude by testifying concerning Jesus as the Christ and the Divine Redeemer. He lives! His are the sweet words of eternal life. He is the Son of the Living God. This is His holy work and glory. This is His church. It is true. I am most grateful for this sacred knowledge. It is my cherished privilege and duty to so testify.

29

STRENGTHENING EACH OTHER

PRESIDENT GORDON B. HINCKLEY

What a wonderful time to be alive! This is the greatest age in the history of the earth in scientific and technological advancement. Additionally, this is the gospel "dispensation of the fulness of times," when all of the power and authority of previous dispensations have been restored to earth. It is a wonderful time to be a member of the Church, with millions of members all belonging to the greatest community of friends in all the world. Wherever one goes as a faithful Latter-day Saint he will have instant friends if he makes his identity known.

When the emperor of Japan visited the United States some years ago, I attended a luncheon for him in San Francisco. I sat at a table with people who were not members of the Church who had lived in Japan where they had known Church members. The topic of conversation drifted to the culture shock experienced by persons who go to live in nations in which they are not reared. A knowledgeable man, who had lived abroad a number of years, said, "I have never seen anything like your people to make others feel comfortable and at home. Whenever a Mormon family came to Japan, a week had not passed before they had many friends. It was different with others. Most of them felt extremely lonely and experienced great difficulty in making adjustments."

Remember, we are not alone. We belong to a great body of friends, thousands upon thousands who are striving to follow the teachings of the Lord. Even so, I know that there are many who are in the minority where they live. Fortunately, however, almost without exception there are Latter-day Saints nearby, people of our own kind with whom we can mingle freely and live the standards we have learned to appreciate.

I remember interviewing a discouraged missionary. He was having trouble with a language which was not his own. He had lost the spirit of his work and wanted to go home. He was one of 180 missionaries in that mission.

I told him that if he were to go home he would break faith with his 179 companions. Every one of them was his friend. Every one of them would pray for him, fast for him, and do almost anything else to help him. They would work with him. They would teach him. They would get on their knees with him. They would help him to learn the language and be successful because they loved him.

I am happy to report that he accepted my assurance that all of the other missionaries were his friends. They rallied around him, not to embarrass him, but to strengthen him. The terrible feeling of loneliness left him. He came to realize that he was part of a winning team. He became successful, a leader, and he has been a leader ever since.

That's what each of us must do for one another.

Paul wrote to the Romans, "We then that are strong ought to bear the infirmities of the weak." And then he added these significant words, "And not to please ourselves." (Romans 15:1.)

There is a sad tendency in our world today for persons to cut one another down. Did you ever realize that it does not take very much in the way of brainpower to make remarks that may wound another? Try the opposite of that. Try handing out compliments.

For a number of years, while I had responsibility for the work in Asia, I interviewed each missionary one-on-one. I asked each what virtue he or she saw in his or her companion and would like to put into his or her own life.

When I raised that question, almost invariably the missionary, an elder for example, would stop with a surprised look on his face. He had never thought of his companion that way before. He had seen his faults and weaknesses but had not seen his virtues. I would tell him to pause and think about it for a minute. Then the answers would begin to come. Such answers as, "He's a hard worker." "He gets up in the morning." "He dresses neatly." "He doesn't complain."

It was a remarkable thing, really. These young men and women, for the most part, had been oblivious to the virtues of their companions, although they were well aware of their companions' faults and often felt discouraged because of them. But when they began to turn their attitudes around, remarkable things began to happen.

I know that each of us gets discouraged on occasion. Most of us feel at one time or another that we have failed. I am confident that the Prophet Joseph Smith felt a sense of failure and sadness when he crossed the Mississippi River to leave his enemies only to learn that some of his own people were saying that he was running away. He replied, "If my life is of no value to my friends it is of none to myself." (*History of the Church*, 6:549.) He returned, and went to Carthage and his death a short time later.

I have seen President David O. McKay discouraged. I have seen President Joseph Fielding Smith and President Harold B. Lee and President Spencer W. Kimball discouraged. All of us can become discouraged. But when I think of discouragement, I sometimes think of a news article I once read:

"If you sometimes get discouraged, consider this fellow. He dropped out of grade school. Ran a country store. Went broke. Took 15 years to pay off his bills. Took a wife. Unhappy marriage. Ran for House. Lost twice. Ran for Senate. Lost twice. Delivered speech that became a classic. Audience indifferent. Attacked daily by the press and despised by half the country. Despite all this, imagine how many people all over the world have been inspired by this awkward, rumpled, brooding man who signed his name simply, A. Lincoln." (*Wall Street Journal,* date unknown.)

It is important to know, when you feel down, that many others do also and that their circumstances are generally much worse than yours. And it's important to know that when one of us is down, it becomes the obligation of his friends to give him a lift. I hope that each of us will cultivate a sensitivity toward the feelings of others, and when encouragement is needed, make an effort to extend it. Be a friend, and you will have a friend. God be thanked for wonderful friends.

There is also in our society a sad tendency among many of us to belittle ourselves. Other persons may appear to us to be sure of themselves, but the fact is that most of us have some feelings of inferiority. The important thing is not to talk to yourself about it. All of us cannot be tall, dark, and handsome. All of us cannot be trim of figure or have a beautiful face. The important thing is to make the best of all that we have.

Don't waste your time feeling sorry for yourself. Don't belittle yourself. Never forget that you are a child of God. You have a divine birthright. Something of the very nature of God is within you. The Psalmist sang, "I have said, Ye are gods; and all of you are children of the most High." (Psalm 82:6.)

I think that David must have been sitting under the stars thinking of this great potential when he wrote: "What is man, that thou art mindful of him? and the son of man, that thou visitest him?

"For thou hast made him a little lower than the angels, and hast crowned him with glory and honour.

"Thou madest him to have dominion over the works of thy hands; thou hast put all things under his feet." (Psalm 8:4-6.)

Each person has the potential for great things. Said the Lord through revelation, "Be thou humble; and the Lord thy God will lead thee by the hand, and give thee answer to thy prayers." (D&C 112:10.) What a marvelous promise that is, and so applicable to our personal development.

There is another trait related to our personal progress about which I would like to comment. In our academically advanced age, one sees much of what I choose to call intellectual arrogance. It is for the most part a false and specious thing. And, because it is a specious thing, it generally gives rise to cynicism and ultimately to discouragement in one form or another.

A Book of Mormon prophet said, "O that cunning plan of the evil one! O the vainness, and the frailties, and the foolishness of men! When they are learned they think they are wise, and they hearken not unto the counsel of God, for they set it aside, supposing they know of themselves, wherefore, their wisdom is foolishness and it profiteth them not. And they shall perish." (2 Nephi 9:28.)

There is an interesting story in the history of the Church. It concerns a man who was great and then fell because he became somewhat arrogant. Concerning him, President Wilford Woodruff said, "I have seen Oliver Cowdery when it seemed as though the earth trembled under his feet. I never heard a man bear a stronger testimony than he did when under the influence of the Spirit. But the moment he left the kingdom of God, that moment his power fell like lightning from heaven. He was shorn of his strength like Samson in the lap of Delilah. He lost the power and the testimony which he had enjoyed, and he never recovered it again in its fulness while in the flesh, although he died in the Church." (As quoted by Stanley R. Gunn, *Oliver Cowdery: Second Elder and Scribe*, Salt Lake City: Bookcraft, 1962, p. 73.)

As the years pass, we each face challenges within ourselves, generally in areas where we need development and refinement. Questions may arise in our minds concerning the Church, its history, its doctrine, its practices. I want to give you my testimony concerning this work. I have been heavily involved in it for more than a half a century. I have worked with the Presidents of the Church from President Heber J. Grant onward. I have known in a very personal way President Grant, President George Albert Smith, President David O. McKay, President Joseph Fielding Smith, President Harold B. Lee, President Spencer W. Kimball, and President Ezra Taft Benson. I have known the counselors of all of these men, and I have known the Council of the Twelve during the years of the administrations of these Presidents. All of these men have been human. They have had human traits and perhaps some human weaknesses. But over and above all of that, there has been in the life of every one of them an overpowering manifestation of the inspiration of God. Those who have been Presidents have been prophets in a very real way. I have intimately witnessed the spirit of revelation upon them. Each man came to the Presidency after many years of experience as a member of the Council of the Twelve and in other capacities. The

Lord refined and polished each one, let him know discouragement and failure, let him experience illness and in some cases deep sorrow. All of this became part of a great refining process, and the effect of that process became beautifully evident in their lives.

This is God's work. This is His Church and the Church of His Beloved Son whose name it carries. God will never permit an imposter to stand at its head. He will name His prophets, and He will inspire and direct them. Joseph Smith was His great prophet in opening this dispensation of the fulness of times. Joyfully and truthfully we can sing, "Praise to the man who communed with Jehovah! Jesus anointed that Prophet and Seer." ("Praise to the Man," *Hymns,* no. 27.)

God bless each of us with faith and with a testimony of this great and holy work. May He also grant joy to each of us through the service we give in the fulfillment of God's plans concerning His great work in these latter days.

The Lord himself has spoken it: "The keys of the kingdom of God are committed unto man on the earth, and from thence shall the gospel roll forth unto the ends of the earth, as the stone which is cut out of the mountain without hands shall roll forth, until it has filled the whole earth." (D&C 65:2.)

WITH GOD NOTHING SHALL BE IMPOSSIBLE

ELDER RUSSELL M. NELSON

I applaud the efforts of Latter-day Saints throughout the world who willingly serve in building the kingdom of God. Likewise, I respect those who quietly do their duty though deepening trials come their way. And I admire those who strive to be more worthy by overcoming a personal fault or who work to achieve a difficult goal.

I feel impressed to counsel those engaged in personal challenges to do right. In particular, my heart reaches out to those who feel discouraged by the magnitude of their struggle. Many shoulder heavy burdens of righteous responsibility that, on occasion, seem so difficult to bear. I have heard those challenges termed *impossible*.

As a medical doctor, I have known the face of adversity. I have seen much of death and dying, suffering and sorrow. I also remember the plight of students overwhelmed by their studies and of those striving to learn a foreign language. And I recall the fatigue and frustration felt by young parents with children in need. Amidst circumstances seemingly impossible, I have also experienced the joyous relief that comes when one's understanding is deepened by scriptural insight.

The Lord has often chosen to instruct His people in

their times of trial. Scriptures show that some of His lasting lessons have been taught with examples terrible as war, commonplace as childbearing, or obvious as hazards of deep water. His teachings are frequently based on common understanding, but with uncommon results. Indeed, one might say that to teach His people, the Lord employs the unlikely.

Warfare, for example, has been known since time began. Even in that ugly circumstance, the Lord has helped those obedient to his counsel. Going into battle, all would assume the obvious advantage of outnumbering an enemy. But when God's disciple Gideon was leading an army against the Midianites, "the Lord said unto Gideon, The people that are with thee are too many . . . , lest Israel vaunt themselves . . . , saying, Mine own hand hath saved me." (Judges 7:2.)

So the Lord directed Gideon to reduce his numbers. He first decreased the troops from twenty-two thousand to ten thousand.

Then the Lord said to Gideon, "The people are yet too many." (Judges 7:4.) So another reduction was made. Finally, only three hundred remained. Then the Lord delivered the victory to the outnumbered few. (See Judges 7:5-25.)

Even more widely known than war is an understanding of childbearing. Everyone "knows" that *old* women do not bear children. So upon whom did the Lord call to bear Abraham's birthright son? Sarah, at age ninety. When told this was to be, she asked a logical question: "Shall I [which am old] of a surety bear a child?" (Genesis 18:13.) From heaven came this reply: "Is any thing too hard for the Lord?" (Genesis 18:14.)

So decreed, she gave birth to Isaac, to carry the crucial

Abrahamic covenant into the second generation. (See Genesis 26:1-4, 24.)

Later, for one of the most important events ever to occur, the other extreme was chosen. As all knew that an elderly woman could not bear children, it was just as obvious that a virgin could not have children. But Isaiah had made this prophetic utterance: "The Lord himself shall give you a sign; Behold, a virgin shall conceive, and bear a son, and shall call his name Immanuel." (Isaiah 7:14.)

When Mary was notified of her sacred responsibility, the announcing angel reassured, "For with God nothing shall be impossible." (Luke 1:37.)

The expression *deep water* means danger! That very hazard challenged the Israelites led by Moses at the Red Sea (see Exodus 14). Later, they were led by Joshua to the river Jordan at flood time (see Joshua 3). In each instance, deep water was divinely divided to allow the faithful to reach their destination safely. To teach His people, the Lord employs the unlikely.

Turning to our day, have you ever wondered why the Master waited so long to inaugurate the promised "restitution of all things"? (Acts 3:21.) Any competitor knows the disadvantage of allowing an opponent to get too far ahead. Wouldn't the work of the restoration of the Church have been easier if begun earlier?

Suppose for a moment you are a member of a team. The coach beckons you from the bench and says: "You are to enter this contest. I not only want you to win; you shall win. But the going will be tough. The score at this moment is 1,143,000,000 to six, and you are to play on the team with the six points."

That large number was the approximate population of the earth in the year 1830 when the restored Church of Jesus Christ was officially organized with six members. (See

James Avery Joyce, sel., *World Population Basic Documents*, 4 vols., Dobbs Ferry, New York: Oceana Publications, Inc., 1976, 4:2214.) The setting was remote and rural. By standards of the world, its leaders were deemed to be unlearned. Their followers seemed so ordinary. But with them, the work was begun. Assignments had been revealed:

• The gospel was to be preached to every kindred, nation, tongue, and people.

• Ordinary folk were to become Saints.

• Redemptive work was to be done for all who had ever lived.

The great dispensation of the latter days had commenced, and they were the ones to usher it forth!

Furthermore, the Prophet Joseph Smith was unjustly held in the unspeakable isolation of a distant prison. In such obscurity, then and there, he was told by the Lord that "the ends of the earth shall inquire after thy name." (D&C 122:1.)

If any tasks ever deserved the label *impossible*, those would seem to qualify. But, in fact, our Lord had spoken: "With men this is impossible; but with God all things are possible." (Matthew 19:26; see also Mark 10:27; Luke 18:27.) To teach His people, the Lord employs the unlikely.

A century and a half later, the burdening baton of that opportunity has now been passed to us. We are children of the noble birthright, who must carry on in spite of our foredetermined status to be broadly outnumbered and widely opposed. Challenges lie ahead for the Church and for each member divinely charged toward self-improvement and service.

How is it possible to achieve the "impossible"? Learn and obey the teachings of God. From the holy scriptures, heaven-sent lift will be found for heaven-sent duties. To so achieve, at least three basic scriptural themes loom repeatedly as requirements.

FAITH

The foremost requisite is *faith*. It is the first principle of the gospel. (See Articles of Faith 1:4.) In his epistle to the Hebrews, Paul so taught. He concluded that by faith the great deeds of Noah, Abraham, Sarah, Isaac, Jacob, Joseph, Moses, Joshua, and others were accomplished. (See Hebrews 11:4-34.)

Prophets on the American hemisphere similarly taught the fundamental importance of faith. Moroni said it included things "hoped for and not seen" and then warned his skeptics, "Dispute not because ye see not, for ye receive no witness until after the trial of your faith." (Ether 12:6.) Then he spoke of leaders whose faith preceded their miraculous deeds, including Alma, Amulek, Nephi, Lehi, Ammon, the brother of Jared, and the three who were promised that they should not taste of death. (See Ether 12:13-20.)

The Lord personally taught this truth to His disciples: "If ye have faith," He said, "nothing shall be impossible unto you." (Matthew 17:20.)

Faith is nurtured through knowledge of God. It comes from prayer and feasting upon the words of Christ through diligent study of the scriptures.

FOCUS

The second requisite I have classified as *focus*. Imagine, if you will, a pair of powerful binoculars. Two separate optical systems are joined together with a gear to focus two independent images into one three-dimensional view. To apply this analogy, let the scene on the left side of your binoculars represent *your perception* of your task. Let the picture on the right side represent the *Lord's perspective* of your task—the portion of His plan He has entrusted to you. Now, connect your system to His. By mental adjustment, fuse your focus. Something wonderful happens. Your vision and His are now the same. You have developed an "eye single to the glory of God." (D&C 4:5; see also Mormon 8:15.) With that perspective, look upward—above and beyond mundane things about you. The Lord said, "Look unto me in every thought." (D&C 6:36.) That special vision will also help clarify your wishes when they may be a bit fuzzy and out of focus with God's hopes for your divine destiny. Indeed, the precise challenge you regard now as "impossible" may be the very refinement you need, in His eye.

I remember visiting the home of a man terminally ill. The stake president introduced me to the man's family. His wife demonstrated such focus when she asked for a blessing for her dying husband—not for healing, but for peace, not for a miracle, but for ability to abide to the end. She could see from an eternal viewpoint, not merely from the perspective of one weighted with the responsibilities of her husband's day-to-day care.

Elsewhere, a mother with focus nurtures her son, crippled for the whole of this life. Daily, she thanks her Heavenly Father for the privilege of laboring in love with a child for whom mortality's vale of tears will be mercifully brief. Her focus is fixed on eternity. With celestial sight, trials impossible to change become possible to endure.

STRENGTH AND COURAGE

A third theme in the scriptures requisite for significant accomplishment is difficult to summarize in one word, so I shall link two to describe it—*strength* and *courage*. Repeatedly, scriptures yoke these attributes of character together, especially when difficult challenges are to be conquered. (See Deuteronomy 31:6, 7, 23; Joshua 1:6, 7, 9, 18; 10:25; 1 Chronicles 22:13; 28:20; 2 Chronicles 32:7; Psalms 27:14; 31:24; Alma 43:43; 53:20.)

Perhaps this is more easily illustrated than defined. Our pioneer forefathers are good examples. They sang, "Gird up your loins; fresh courage take." ("Come, Come, Ye Saints," *Hymns,* no. 30.) They feared no toil and no labor. Among them were Johan Andreas Jensen and his wife, Petra, who left their native Norway in 1863. Their family included six-week-old tiny twin daughters. As handcarts were pulled in their rugged journey, one of those little girls died along the way. The child who survived grew up to become my Grandmother Nelson.

There are pioneers in the Church today just as strong and courageous. Recently, I interviewed a married couple three days after their release as full-time missionaries in a large metropolis. "We are converts," they said. "We joined the Church ten years ago. Even though we just completed a mission, we want to go again. But this time, we would like to volunteer for a more difficult assignment. We want to teach and serve children of God who live in remote areas of the world."

As I countered with the grim realities of their request, they continued their expression of commitment. "Our three children and their spouses will assist with our expenses. Two of those couples have joined the Church already, and the third is equally supportive. Please send us among humble people who love the Lord and desire to know that His Church has again been restored to the earth." Needless to say, their petition was gratefully heard, and now they have received their second call to missionary service.

Strength and courage also characterize another couple. As faithful members of the Church, they had always upheld its doctrines, including the twelfth article of faith. When their country went to war, military conscription called the dutiful husband away from his wife before either had learned she was to bear their child. He was captured by enemy troops and taken as a prisoner of war. Months elapsed. Their baby came. Still no word to know whether the new father was alive. A year after his capture, he was permitted to write to his wife.

Meanwhile, though countries apart, they each remained faithful to covenants made at baptism. Even though clothed in prisoner's stripes and able to speak the language of his captors' country only in a limited way, he became Sunday School superintendent of the branch. He baptized four fellow prisoners during their confinement. Three years after the war ended, he returned home to his wife and a son he had never seen. Later, he served for ten years as the first stake president of his country. Now he is a member of the presidency of one of our temples. His wife stands faithfully beside him in the privilege of that sacred assignment.

You who may be momentarily disheartened, remember, life is not meant to be easy. Trials must be borne and grief endured along the way. As you remember that "with God nothing shall be impossible" (Luke 1:37), know that He is your Father. You are a son or daughter created in His image, entitled through your worthiness to receive revelation to help with your righteous endeavors. You may take upon you the holy name of the Lord. You can qualify to speak in the sacred name of God. (See D&C 1:20.) It matters not that giants of tribulation torment you. Your prayerful access to help is just as real as when David battled his Goliath. (See 1 Samuel 17.)

Foster your faith. Fuse your focus with an eye single to the glory of God. "Be strong and courageous" (2 Chronicles 32:7), and you will be given power and protection from on high. "For I will go before your face," the Lord declared. "I will be on your right hand and on your left, and my Spirit shall be in your hearts, and mine angels round about you, to bear you up." (D&C 84:88.)

The great latter-day work of which we are a part shall be accomplished. Prophecies of the ages shall be fulfilled. "For with God all things are possible." (Mark 10:27.)

THERE IS ALWAYS HOPE

ELDER JOHN H. GROBERG

There is always hope. No matter how dismal things appear, no matter how problem-prone we seem to be, no matter what reversals and setbacks we suffer, there is always hope. Hope is the thing that keeps us going. We sing the hymn "We Thank Thee, O God, for a Prophet" all the time, but do we listen to the words? What do you feel when you sing, "When dark clouds of trouble hang o'er us And threaten our peace to destroy, There is hope smiling brightly before us, And we know that deliverance is nigh"? (*Hymns*, no. 19.) Do we really believe that?

Part of the thirteenth article of faith reads, "We believe all things, we hope all things, we have endured many things, and hope to be able to endure all things." Do we really believe that? Are we literally supposed to hope all things?

What do we mean by hope? What is hope? Why should we have hope? What do we hope for? What are some of the signs of true hope? How do we get more hope?

HOPE IS LIGHT

What is hope? Like trying to define faith or love, this is very difficult. But we can use some examples. As near as I can tell, hope is light. It is a light within us that pierces

46

the darkness of doubt and discouragement and taps into the light (hope) of all creation—even the Savior.

In some instances we may be able to substitute the word *hope* for *light* and get some understanding in the scriptures. For example, we talk about Christ as being the light of the world—He is the hope of the world. (See Mosiah 16:9.)

The Lord sent the everlasting gospel to be a light unto the Gentiles—to be a hope to the Gentiles. (See Acts 13:47.) The Spirit giveth light to every man—the Spirit giveth hope to every man. (See D&C 84:46.) Christ is the true light that is in all men—Christ is the true hope that is in all men. (See D&C 88:50.)

You will have to think of your own definition, but consider this scriptural explanation: "And if your eye be single to my glory, your whole bodies shall be filled with light [be filled with hope], and there shall be no darkness in you [no discouragement]; and that body which is filled with light [filled with hope] comprehendeth all things." (D&C 88:67.) Isn't that what the article of faith says, we hope all things?

Hope, in a word, is the Savior. Hope is a part of the deity in us that attaches us to the Savior. Don't let that thread be cut. No matter how tenuous or thin it might be, there is always hope.

WE HAVE NEED FOR HOPE

Where does hope come from? Why should we have hope? Why do we keep on hoping even after we blow our diet or get a bad grade or lose a close game or get turned down in some way or another?

In all ages of time and in all dispensations, people have felt a need for hope. There is a saying—a proverb—in Tongan that goes, "*'Ikai ke 'i ai ha mamahi hange ha 'amanaki to noa.*" That means, "There is no pain so great as a hope unfulfilled."

I'm sure if I were familiar with other cultures—French or Russian or Chinese or others—there would be something similar, because hope is in all people.

HOPE IS ETERNAL

Why do we keep on hoping? It is said that "hope springs eternal," and it's good it does, for it gives us something to live for, to strive for, to hope for. But why? Why does hope spring eternal? Why do we keep coming back and back after so many defeats? Simply because God is eternal and God is hope (as well as love—and they may be the same) and we are His children. Therefore, as He is the embodiment of hope and has a fullness of hope, there is planted deep within each of us something we cannot deny, for it is part of the very essence of ourselves; and that is what we call, in mortality, hope.

A person without hope is like a person without a heart; there is nothing to keep him going. As the heart gives life to the body, so it seems that hope is an enlivening influence to the spirit—which is the real us. No matter what people try to say, it's always there—that hope is within us. But how brightly will we allow it to shine in our lives? The degree of "shining" (or the strength) of this hope that is in all of us is in direct proportion to our faith in God and particularly to our faith in (belief in, love of, hope in) Jesus Christ. Specifically, then, the basis of all righteous hope is the person of our Lord and Savior Jesus Christ. In Him all hope has its existence. Without Him there is no hope. But because He was and is and ever will be, there was, is, and ever will be hope—hope in all areas. He is hope.

WE ALL HOPE FOR DIFFERENT THINGS

What do we hope for? Maybe you hope to lose weight, or maybe you hope your children will turn out okay or you

48

will get a good job offer, or you hope you will have good health or better health. We all hope for different things at different times, depending on our maturity level—all the way from an infant hoping for a bottle to a student hoping for good grades to an adult hoping for love and understanding. Ultimately, we all hope for the greatest of all gifts—immortality and eternal life. In fact, in order to have a true saving hope, that hope must transcend this mortal sphere.

So what do we hope for? Remember the article of faith? All things. Listen to the words of Moroni:

"And again, my beloved brethren, I would speak unto you concerning hope. How is it that ye can attain unto faith, save ye shall have hope?

"And what is it that ye shall hope for? Behold I say unto you that ye shall have hope through the atonement of Christ and the power of his resurrection, to be raised unto life eternal, and this because of your faith in him according to the promise.

"Wherefore, if a man have faith he must needs have hope; for without faith there cannot be any hope.

"And again, behold I say unto you that he cannot have faith and hope, save he shall be meek, and lowly of heart.

"If so, his faith and hope is vain, for none is acceptable before God, save the meek and lowly in heart; and if a man be meek and lowly in heart, and confesses by the power of the Holy Ghost that Jesus is the Christ, he must needs have charity; for if he have not charity he is nothing; wherefore he must needs have charity." (Moroni 7:40-44.)

THERE ARE SIGNS OF TRUE HOPE

What are some of the signs of true hope? Calmness, optimism, or all those things that are the opposite of down-heartedness or being disturbed. You can almost measure the level of hope you have in the Savior by the depth and frequency of depression and discouragement you allow yourself to sink into.

Just as discouragement and depression feed on themselves (Can't you just hear Satan saying, "You can't do it, you are no good, you'll never make it"—sometimes he says that right to your heart, and sometimes he uses others as his agents), so does hope regenerate itself. Can't you likewise hear the Savior saying, "You can do it, you can make it, you are worth something. I laid down my life for you. I love you. I redeemed you. I paid for you because I know you can make it. You can come home. Trust me. Follow me." Sometimes He speaks directly to our hearts and sometimes He uses others as His agents. But there is always hope in Him.

Another sign of true hope is that we don't judge other people—including ourselves. I often hear people talk of hope in another sense. They say, "Well, I hope he gets what's coming," or, "I hope justice is done." Don't worry about that. He or she will. The ones we ought to worry about are ourselves.

We spend so much time and effort seeking remedies or justice (on spiritual things especially) "here and now" when, in fact, much, if not most, of justice will be done "there and then." We ought to spend time and effort here and now to prepare for there and then. Probably most "justice" occurs after this life. We ought to be glad it does, for so much went on before and will go on after of which we are not aware—but God is aware.

If we are to have a fullness of hope (and that is our goal—hope all things), our hope must transcend this mortal existence. It had better, for as Paul indicated, "If in this life only we have hope in Christ, we are of all men most miserable." (1 Corinthians 15:19.) One who has a true hope in Christ will not judge others.

From a remarkable talk given by President Stephen L

Richards in April 1956, I quote: "The Lord has said, 'I, the Lord, will forgive whom I will forgive, but of you it is required to forgive all men.' (D&C 64:10.) If we were more liberal in our forgiveness, we would be more encouraging to repentance. Someone has said that the supreme charity of the world is in obedience to the divine injunction, 'Judge not.' When the Savior gave that injunction, he was well aware of the limitations of human understanding and sympathy. We can see overt acts, but we cannot see inner feelings nor can we read intentions. An all-wise Providence in making judgment sees and knows all the phases of human conduct. We know but few of the phases, and none very well. To be considerate and kind in judgment is a Christlike attribute." ("Encouragement for Repenters," *Improvement Era*, June 1956, p. 399.)

Those with hope, then, do not judge. When I hear of people making judgments (and we all do more than we want to—we do too much) I think, "Who do we think we are anyway? The very best of us, the most kind or most loving and forgiving among us, is only, as it were, in kindergarten— or lower."

Let me read something on this point written by Elder Orson F. Whitney some years ago: "You parents of the wilful and the wayward: Don't give them up. Don't cast them off. They are not utterly lost. The Shepherd will find his sheep. They were his before they were yours—long before he entrusted them to your care; and you cannot begin to love them as he loves them. Our Heavenly Father is far more merciful, infinitely more charitable, than even the best of his servants, and the Everlasting Gospel is mightier in power to save than our narrow finite minds can comprehend."

It is important to follow the admonition given by King Benjamin in Mosiah 4:9: "Believe in God; believe that he is, and that he created all things, both in heaven and in earth; believe that he has all wisdom, and all power, both in heaven and in earth; believe that man doth not comprehend all the things which the Lord can comprehend [sometimes we, by our actions and our requests, indicate that we think we are smarter than He is]."

Let's not spend our time hoping or worrying about justice being done to others. It will be done. Let's spend our time just being ourselves.

One of Satan's ultimate weapons (if not the ultimate) is to remove hope from your life. He tries to convince you that you can't do it, that there is no hope. Thus, by removing hope, he removes Christ from your life, for Christ is hope. Satan can never quite accomplish that fully—at least not here—because it is a lie. There is hope built within all of us. There is always hope.

On the other hand, the thing Satan cannot fight is one who is full of hope—for he is then full of the Spirit of Christ—and when that hope is perfected or full, Satan has lost completely.

Another sign of having hope is the encouragement we give others. Let me assure you that if by our words or our actions or by our very being we tell people (or even give the impression), "You can't do it, you are no good, you'll never measure up, you'll never make it," or (maybe worst of all) "I won't forgive you" (and all of these things apply doubly to our reaction to ourselves and to our own faults), then we are moving away from God and not toward Him, for He gives hope and says, "There is always hope." Don't ever say there isn't.

If we, to others or to ourselves, fail to give full measure of hope (remember the scripture, full measure, pressed down and overflowing), we do less than Jesus would do and less than He would have us do. (See Luke 6:38.)

Now, as in all things, to receive anything good we must

give it away. Maybe the reason we don't have more hope is because we don't give enough hope to others. If we want more hope, let's give more hope to others — be more encouraging.

The spirit of hope is the Spirit of the Savior. He is always encouraging.

Now you might say, "Okay, I believe that. Doctrinally it's correct, but what does it mean to me? I want more hope. How do I get more? If it's there, if it is within me (and it is), how do I allow it to shine forth and fill my life and move me forward in this light of hope?"

Consider two verses from the Book of Mormon:

"And the remission of sins bringeth meekness, and lowliness of heart; and because of meekness and lowliness of heart cometh the visitation of the Holy Ghost, which Comforter filleth with hope and perfect love, which love endureth by diligence unto prayer, until the end shall come, when all the saints shall dwell with God." (Moroni 8:26.)

"Wherefore, ye must press forward with a steadfastness in Christ, having a perfect brightness of hope, and a love of God and of all men. Wherefore, if ye shall press forward, feasting upon the word of Christ [which are the scriptures, of course], and endure to the end, behold, thus saith the Father: Ye shall have eternal life." (2 Nephi 31:20.) And isn't that what we are hoping for?

Those two key verses explain so clearly what we need to do. The key elements are repentance, remission of sins, meekness, lowliness of heart, love of God and of all men, feasting on the words of Christ, studying the scriptures, praying, enduring to the end — quite opposite from some of the success formulas in the world.

As near as I can tell, if you don't have hope, you either don't have the Holy Ghost or you aren't listening to him, for it states clearly, "which Comforter filleth with hope and perfect love."

PRESS FORWARD

The scriptures talk about a "perfect brightness of hope." Think about that. Wouldn't you like to have that — to never be down, never be discouraged? That would be great, wouldn't it? I think all of us would agree. But will it ever happen here? Like a lot of things, it is difficult, but it can happen, else why the injunction from the Lord to Nephi to "press forward with a steadfastness in Christ, having a perfect brightness of hope, and a love of God and of all men"? (2 Nephi 31:20.)

But like anything else good, it is not easy, it does not come without effort. Satan will try to diminish your hope or keep it away from you altogether if he can. The Savior will help you increase in hope.

So you see, the battle lines are clearly drawn. Satan and his forces (the world) will do everything in their power to have you lose hope — to be constantly down on yourself, always discouraged, despondent, and so forth. Satan wants to discourage you, for he knows discouragement and hope cannot exist together.

On the other hand, the Savior will do just the opposite. He will do all in His power to encourage you, lift you up, give you hope, help you in every way possible, so that with a "steadfastness in Christ" you may attain to that "perfect brightness of hope." Then discouragement and despair are gone.

Darkness, discouragement, pessimism, depression, anger, lack of hope — all come from Satan and his forces. Optimism, light, encouragement, hope, even to a perfect brightness of hope — all come from the Savior.

Now some may say, "Well, you are bordering on calling

discouragement a sin, and we know that we all get discouraged sometimes. It's just human nature."

True enough, it's human nature. All humans get discouraged at times. All humans die sometime, too. But through the Savior we will overcome death and through Him we must overcome discouragement as well. And we can.

RELY ON THE SAVIOR

Those of the world are betting that this life is it. You have heard the statement, "Better red than dead." That is all based on the assumption that there is nothing after this life. To them, there is no hope for the future. To them it's eat, drink, and be merry, and get what you can, when you can, how you can. That is not true. Hope is available. Hope is here. Hope (and this is really hope in Christ) is the essence of life.

To say "There is no hope for me" is to say there is no Savior, for He is hope and He does exist, so there is hope for you. He is forever, so there is always hope.

Basically, those without hope are those who rely only on themselves, those who have not tapped into that power beyond themselves, even the Savior Himself—and there are far too many in the world today who rely totally on themselves. While it is good to be self-reliant, you have to rely on yourself and on the Savior.

The Savior came to the earth to do several things—to fulfill the plan made in heaven before the earth was, to do the will of the Father, to work out the infinite Atonement, to break the bands of death and become the first fruits of the resurrection, to fulfill all prophecy, and so on. I wonder if all that He came to do couldn't be summed up in the phrase, "He came to give us hope. He came to show us that indeed there is always hope." For He is always, and He is hope.

Is there anything more universal than a need for hope? We all do things wrong; we need hope to have them taken from us. We all have problems; we need hope that they will go away. If there were not hope, we would be lost forever.

Think of the hope that genealogy and temple work give us and millions of others. Think of the total depth and breadth the hope of the Savior gives us in the gospel plan. You just can't comprehend it. Remember, we hope all things. Do we? The gospel is hope-giving.

I hear some people say, "The gospel is too restrictive." But we must look at the other side. It is really not restrictive at all. It is hope-giving. It gives us a pattern to follow whereby we can gain hope. There is hope, and that is what the Church is about. That is what the Savior is about. He came to give us hope.

We must change, and we can. The message of the gospel of Jesus Christ is, "I can change; there is always hope." We can choose and improve and become as He is.

Remember the quotation from 1 John 3:2-3: "Beloved, now are we the sons of God, and it doth not yet appear what we shall be: but we know that, when he shall appear, we shall be like him; for we shall see him as he is. And every man that hath this hope in him purifieth himself, even as he is pure."

Hope is a purifying, refining process.

THE ATONEMENT IS FOR EVERYONE

How do I know there is hope for all? Because it was a universal atonement. As the scriptures tell us, "For behold, I, God, have suffered these things for all, that they might not suffer if they would repent." (D&C 19:16.) That is, there was no holding back on the Savior's part. He paid the full price for all—full measure, pressed down, overflowing.

56

President Spencer W. Kimball said: "I want to be sure that I am well understood. The Lord said, 'Wherefore all manner of sins shall be forgiven unto men, except the sinning against the Holy Ghost and the committing of murder.' (See Matthew 12:31.) None of us will commit sin against the Holy Ghost (generally we do not know enough), and few of us will ever be involved in a murder. Therefore, the sins of mankind can be forgiven. But not by ignoring them; one must go to the proper ecclesiastical officials and clear his problems." (Amsterdam Area Conference, August 1976, p. 4.)

Well, then, if there is always hope, and I, or we, or any of us don't have much hope, how do we go about getting more hope? That is what we really want to know. You pray for it, you ask for it, you listen to your leaders, you follow them, you repent, you serve others, you read the scriptures, and according to the scriptures you become meek and lowly in heart. There is good reason for feasting upon the words of Christ. There is not a single situation you or I can become involved in for which the principle for resolving it is not contained in the scriptures. Read about the life and acts of the Savior—the things He did. If He is hope, then certainly what He did should give hope to us or help us discover the hope within ourselves.

THE SAVIOR IS OUR EXEMPLAR

Let me give a few examples from the Savior's life that cover some of the situations in which we need hope.

You are familiar with the incident of the people bringing the man who was sick with palsy to Christ. But they couldn't get to the Savior, so they let him down through the roof. The Savior healed him because of the great faith—the great hope—that those around him had. (See Luke 5:18-26.)

There is a lesson to learn here. It wasn't easy. They had

to put forth some effort when they let him down through the ceiling. If we want a blessing from hope that is based on having strong faith and strong hope, then we must be prepared to overcome some obstacles, because our hope isn't sufficient to receive the blessing that we hope for.

Consider the story told in Matthew 9:18-26:

"While he spake these things unto them, behold, there came a certain ruler, and worshipped him, saying, My daughter is even now dead: but come and lay thy hand upon her, and she shall live.

"And Jesus arose, and followed him, and so did his disciples.

"And, behold, a woman, which was diseased with an issue of blood twelve years, came behind him, and touched the hem of his garment:

"For she said within herself, If I may but touch his garment, I shall be whole.

"But Jesus turned him about, and when he saw her, he said, Daughter, be of good comfort; thy faith hath made thee whole. And the woman was made whole from that hour.

"And when Jesus came into the ruler's house, and saw the minstrels and the people making a noise,

"He said unto them, Give place: for the maid is not dead, but sleepeth. And they laughed him to scorn.

"But when the people were put forth, he went in, and took her by the hand, and the maid arose.

"And the fame thereof went abroad into all that land."

In Christ there is always hope.

"And they came to Jericho: and as he went out of Jericho with his disciples and a great number of people, blind Bartimaeus, the son of Timaeus, sat by the highway side begging.

"And when he heard that it was Jesus of Nazareth, he

began to cry out, and say, Jesus, thou Son of David, have mercy on me.

"And many charged him that he should hold his peace: but he cried the more a great deal, Thou Son of David, have mercy on me.

"And Jesus stood still, and commanded him to be called. And they call the blind man, saying unto him, Be of good comfort, rise; he calleth thee.

"And he, casting away his garment, rose, and came to Jesus.

"And Jesus answered and said unto him, What wilt thou that I should do unto thee? The blind man said unto him, Lord, that I might receive my sight.

"And Jesus said unto him, Go thy way; thy faith hath made thee whole. And immediately he received his sight, and followed Jesus in the way." (Mark 10:46-52.)

Isn't that the point? In Christ there is always hope.

Another illustration is found in Luke 7:36-47:

"And one of the Pharisees desired him that he would eat with him. And he went into the Pharisee's house, and sat down to meat.

"And, behold, a woman in the city, which was a sinner, when she knew that Jesus sat at meat in the Pharisee's house, brought an alabaster box of ointment,

"And stood at his feet behind him weeping, and began to wash his feet with tears, and did wipe them with the hairs of her head, and kissed his feet, and anointed them with the ointment.

"Now when the Pharisee which had bidden him saw it, he spake within himself, saying, This man, if he were a prophet, would have known who and what manner of woman this is that toucheth him: for she is a sinner.

"And Jesus answering said unto him, Simon, I have somewhat to say unto thee. And he saith, Master, say on.

"There was a certain creditor which had two debtors: the one owed five hundred pence, and the other fifty.

"And when they had nothing to pay, he frankly forgave them both. Tell me therefore, which of them will love him most?

"Simon answered and said, I suppose that he, to whom he forgave most. And he said unto him, Thou hast rightly judged.

"And he turned to the woman, and said unto Simon, Seest thou this woman? I entered into thine house, thou gavest me no water for my feet: but she hath washed my feet with tears, and wiped them with the hairs of her head.

"Thou gavest me no kiss: but this woman since the time I came in hath not ceased to kiss my feet.

"My head with oil thou didst not anoint: but this woman hath anointed my feet with ointment.

"Wherefore I say unto thee, Her sins, which are many, are forgiven; for she loved much: but to whom little is forgiven, the same loveth little."

She hoped. Her hope was rewarded. In Christ there is always hope. I am sure she did more than hope. She changed, and we must also.

Consider another example from the New Testament, from Luke 22:54-62. Remember Peter, the great stalwart apostle, and the problems he had to begin with:

"Then took they him, and led him, and brought him into the high priest's house. And Peter followed afar off.

"And when they had kindled a fire in the midst of the hall, and were set down together, Peter sat down among them.

"But a certain maid beheld him as he sat by the fire, and earnestly looked upon him, and said, This man was also with him.

"And he denied him, saying, Woman, I know him not.

"And after a little while another saw him, and said, Thou art also of them. And Peter said, Man, I am not.

"And about the space of one hour after another confidently affirmed, saying, Of a truth this fellow also was with him: for he is a Galilaean.

"And Peter said, Man, I know not what thou sayest. And immediately, while he yet spake, the cock crew.

"And the Lord turned, and looked upon Peter. And Peter remembered the word of the Lord, how he had said unto him, Before the cock crow, thou shalt deny me thrice.

"And Peter went out, and wept bitterly."

Think about it. How could you feel worse — denying the Savior? How could you be more discouraged? How then did Peter come back and become the strength that he was? Some might imagine that there would have been a look of anguish or distrust on the Savior's face as He looked at Peter at that critical moment; but while there can be sternness in the Savior, the Savior I know is a kind, smiling, helpful Savior — one who constantly encourages. And He did thus with Peter. His look to Peter said: "Come to me. Come home to hope. You know better. You can do better. You will do better. There is always hope. There is always hope in me."

Peter came back and was strong — what a strength he was! And we must come back and be strong. He didn't allow discouragement to overwhelm him. He grasped that hope in the Savior and held onto it until it became a "perfect brightness of hope." And so must we.

Some may say, "Sure, but that was Peter and the Savior, and that was two thousand years ago. I am me and my problems are mine. I live now and He isn't around. I can't touch the hem of His robe. No one understands my problems. My problems are different."

To those comments I say, "He isn't around — oh, isn't

He? No one understands—oh, doesn't He? My problems are different—oh, are they?"

OUR DAY IS NO DIFFERENT

Time is measured only to man, not to God. Life is all one great "now" to Him. This century is no different than A.D. 31. We have essentially the same problems and feelings as those living in Palestine two millennia ago. We might worry about an atomic holocaust rather than Roman legions, but the threat is the same. His Spirit is just as present, He understands just as much, He is as loving and kind and anxious to help as He ever has been. And miracles (if you want to call them that—they are really just His power manifested among men) today are just as real and evident as they have ever been, for faith is among the children of men. Hope is among the children of men. You may question that. Don't. It's true.

Let me give you just one example in our day. I am going to use this as a sort of composite so that no one will identify it with one particular person. All the incidents that I'll mention are true, but there were three different people involved.

THERE IS POWER IN HOPE

Shortly after I was called to be a General Authority, I was asked to interview a young girl who wanted to go on a mission. She had had some problems. When we went over all the problems that she had, I thought to myself, "What is she doing here? There is no way a girl with all these problems can go on a mission." But there was something radiant about her honesty. She didn't hold anything back. She was completely honest, and I could sense that she had real hope. She really wanted to go on a mission.

I wanted to just say no. I had been a mission president,

and I thought I wouldn't have wanted someone with that kind of record in my mission. But there was something that said, "Wait a while." So I didn't say no. I said, "Why don't you come back next week? Let's pray about it and think about it." I was planning to tell her no.

Shortly after that I learned that my next stake conference assignment had been changed. I was to go someplace else.

I went to this other place. My plane arrived a little before we needed to be in meetings. The stake president picked me up. He said, "We're having a family reunion, and that is where we are going to have lunch."

I said, "Fine."

We went out to the family reunion. As we ate, some of the older members of the family gave reports about their families.

The president said, "Well, it is time to go. We had better leave."

Just as he said that, a lady stood up. I said, "I hate to walk out when someone is talking. Let's just wait until she is through."

He said, "Okay, but that is Aunt Cloe and she might talk for a long time."

I said, "Let's see."

She gave a report of her family, and then she said, "And as all of you know, we have had a lot of heartache and trouble with my granddaughter, so-and-so." The name rang a bell. I realized it was the same girl I had just interviewed about going on a mission. She said, "But we are so hopeful. We have heard that she is actually thinking of going on a mission, and, oh, we hope she will be able to go."

As the tears came down this grandmother's face, I realized that I was the one who had to make that decision. I couldn't help but think how powerful the hope of a young girl and her grandmother and probably her mother was. Powerful enough to get my schedule switched around so that I got sent where I could sit down and listen to that grandmother.

Of course, you know what happened. The girl came back the next week and I said, "We will give it a try. You have a lot of hope. You have a lot going for you." What she had going for her was that she wanted to go.

I kept in close touch with her stake president. She served a wonderful mission—a tremendous mission. I would call regularly, or he would call me and say, "I got a letter and things are going fine."

But shortly before she was to come home, I got a call from the stake president.

"Elder Groberg, I have some bad news."

"Oh, no, what?"

"Our friend is home—excommunicated." One month before her mission was up.

She was a determined and repentant girl, and she came in to apologize to me. "I blew it. I am sorry."

The feeling I had when I talked to her was, "Don't forget, there is always hope. Keep trying."

There were so many problems, you can't imagine—a change of mission president, a change of stake president, papers getting lost. Years went by, but I kept in touch. Little by little, things came together. She married a fine young man. And not very long ago I had the opportunity of sealing her and her husband and two little children. It took years, and there was a lot of pain, but as I looked down upon that beautiful tearstained face so full of joy and love and hope, I softly breathed those beautiful words that had meant so much to us for so long: "You see, there is always hope."

THERE ARE MIRACLES IN ALL AGES

You think you are so different. You think your problems evade solution. You think the Savior and His works and love belong to a different time and place? No, they are here now. They have been and ever will be available to all men and women everywhere, regardless of the complexity, the severity, the terribleness, the duration, or the supposed depth of the problem. There is always hope. In Christ who lives and loves and works miracles now, there is always hope. Listen again and again and again. There is always hope—now, today. There is always hope. He lives. He loves. He saves. In Him there is always hope.

What would life be like without hope? Terrible. We can't conceive of it. Remove the Savior from your life and you remove hope. But we can't, and we won't. He is there and He will always whisper to us and assure us. We just simply have to have hope.

Read again the words of Moroni: "Wherefore, there must be faith; and if there must be faith there must also be hope; and if there must be hope there must also be charity.

"And except ye have charity ye can in nowise be saved in the kingdom of God; neither can ye be saved in the kingdom of God if ye have not faith; neither can ye if ye have no hope.

"And if ye have no hope ye must needs be in despair; and despair cometh because of iniquity." (Moroni 10:20-22.)

No matter what price we have to pay, or how long we must suffer, there is always hope. No matter how deep the wound, how dark the night, keep up hope. It is worth it. There is always hope!

No matter the fasting, the struggling, the praying, the weeping, the searching, the confessing. No matter the so-called embarrassment or loss of face or pride or whatever other terms or feelings Satan uses in his attempt to dissuade us from obtaining that saving hope and from securing that glorious hope in the Savior. It is worth it.

"Wherefore, whoso believeth in God might with surety hope for a better world, yea, even a place at the right hand of God, which hope cometh of faith, maketh an anchor to the souls of men, which would make them sure and steadfast, always abounding in good works, being led to glorify God.

"And I also remember that thou hast said that thou hast prepared a house for man, yea, even among the mansions of thy Father, in which man might have a more excellent hope; wherefore man must hope, or he cannot receive an inheritance in the place which thou hast prepared." (Ether 12:4, 32.)

THERE IS ALWAYS HOPE

Remember, there is always hope, for you and for others. The Savior paid the price for all. "For behold, I, God, have suffered these things for all, that they might not suffer if they would repent." (D&C 19:16.)

That's quite inclusive. The Savior was, in our vernacular today, a great optimist, wasn't He? Actually, He was full of hope, or had a fullness of hope. As far as I know, there is not a thing you will do (except sinning against the Holy Ghost or committing murder) that is not covered by the love and the atoning sacrifice of the Savior — nothing. That ought to give you hope, hadn't it?

Stephen L Richards said: "Let no brother or sister in the whole family of God feel that he or she has gone beyond the point where error and sin may be left behind and true repentance enlighten the soul with hope and faith." (Conference Report, 8 April 1956, p. 93.)

You see, there is always hope.

I hope by now we are all beginning to really feel, and

I mean feel and sense deep in our eternal souls, the truth of that marvelous phrase, "There is always hope." I know there is because of the Savior, our Lord and Friend, even Jesus Christ.

To all those who ask the plaintive question, "Is there any hope for me?" the answer is a resounding, "Yes! There is always hope." Reverberating through all eternity, all creation exults: "In Christ there is always hope."

Seek after Him in all ways and at all times until you can sense His smiling countenance saying to you, "Come unto me and I will give you rest. I am the hope of the world. In me there is always hope."

I know that God lives and loves us. I know that Jesus Christ is His Son. I have hope in Christ—a sure hope. You can have one, too. I know He lives, I know He smiles. I know He always gives hope. I know that miracles not only occurred two thousand years ago, but similar manifestations of faith and hope have and will continue to bring down the blessings of heaven on the heads of those faithful, as needed. There is reason and justification for the hope that is within me and should be within all of us.

I testify of Him. I have heard his voice on many occasions in my heart. I have felt His precious presence at various times and in divers places. I have seen His influence over and over again, and I have witnessed His power and majesty as He continues to work His miracles among the children of men in our day—largely through the hope that emanates from Him and to Him and through Him and around Him and by Him through all eternity.

I know by the sure witness of the Spirit that He lives and loves and forgives and heals and saves and restores. In Him there is always hope.

May our hope in Him ever be vibrant and active and sure—"unto a perfect brightness of hope."

Seek Higher Flight Levels

ELDER ROBERT E. WELLS

There are laws irrevocably decreed in the heavens before the foundation of the earth upon which all blessings are predicated. When we receive a blessing, it is because we are obeying those laws. (See D&C 130:20.) There are some laws which are apparently higher in a certain sense than others.

Let me start with a physical law—the law of gravity. If I drop something heavier than air, it falls to the earth. I have been flying small aircraft for some forty years. Aircraft are heavier than air. Some are heavier than cars, some heavier than locomotives. They fly because of a higher law—the law of aerodynamics, the law involving a certain amount of speed coupled with the shape of the lifting surface to overcome gravity. In a sense, it is a higher law.

I fly two kinds of airplanes: those that can cruise anyplace between sea level and about the height of the Rocky Mountains, and those with more powerful engines that can fly above the weather. It is not a pleasant experience to struggle along in bad weather in the kind of aircraft that does not have the power to go up on top. You are there in the dark clouds, the turbulence, the lightning, the thunder, the rain, the hail. It is a beautiful experience, however, to fly a powerful aircraft that will climb quickly through the weather and clouds. As you break through on top, there is glorious, beautiful sunshine and blue sky. And looking down, that which just moments before was dark and threatening is now just lovely and delightful white cloud tops.

SEEK HIGHER LEVELS OF LIFE

Let's apply the concept of climbing above the turbulence to life: Seek the higher flight levels of life. There are many circumstances in our lives. Some of you may think you are as high as you need to go. I am aware of a returned missionary who thinks he has already achieved a superbly high spiritual level. He probably thinks the rest of his life will be anti-climactic. Not so! We should all strive continually for a higher flight level.

There are those recently married who are enjoying the beautiful new love of their lives. Yet they can look forward to even higher levels of loving and living. There are those who are successful in any field—the businessman, the graduate. And there are those who are not enjoying so much success. There is the scholar who didn't get the scholarship. There is the beauty pageant contestant who didn't make it to the finals. There are those who feel they are too tall or too short, too thin or too fat. There are those who are not quite satisfied with all of these circumstances in their lives. There are the lonely, the lost, the disappointed, the hurt, the wounded. All may find a way to the higher levels of life so they can be above the storms of discouragement and dismay. All can climb to higher levels.

GOD GAVE US HIGHER COMMANDMENTS

Let me illustrate some of the higher commandments of life as I feel they were explained by the Savior. The Savior, in the Sermon on the Mount, used the illustration of higher flight levels, or principles. Allow me to make some liberal translations of the scriptures.

In the Sermon on the Mount the Savior might have said, "Thou hast heard from the prophets of old, thou shalt not kill. But allow me to give unto thee a higher law — the law of fellowship, the law of brotherhood. Be not even angry with thy brother." (Cf. Matthew 5:21-22.) This is a higher concept that has the power to lift us above the storms, the turbulences, the trials, and the tribulations of life.

We all know of the additional interpretations of anger — that of being offended, that of criticizing others, that of being bitter. Any of these feelings are like poison to our spirit. The classic illustration is the case of a rattlesnake. If a rattlesnake comes and bites us, what should we do? Should we look for a stick to punish the rattlesnake, or should we try to get the poison out?

Any negative feelings tend to keep us in lower levels of life. We must lift and free ourselves from those things and truly live the spirit of brotherhood and love. Perhaps you have been a roommate or a missionary companion and have experienced the silent treatment or have given the silent treatment. Lift yourself to a higher level of relationship with others.

The Savior might have said, "Thou hast heard from the prophets of old, thou shalt not commit adultery. Allow me to give you a higher law. Thou shalt not even look at a person of the opposite sex to lust after them lest thou hast committed adultery in thy heart." (Cf. Matthew 5:27-28.) He was looking ahead perhaps to this day and age where there is lustful looking, where there are improper magazines and inappropriate movies. Lift yourself to a higher level. It is possible to become addicted. Learn to control thoughts. Learn also that virtue and chastity can be lost piecemeal, a little bit at a time, by lack of thought control, by lack of proper understanding of this higher law of the Savior.

The Savior said, "Thou hast heard from the prophets of old, thou shalt not forswear thyself. But I say unto you, swear not at all. Let your language be, 'Yea, yea' and 'Nay, nay.' " (Cf. Matthew 5:33-37.)

President Heber J. Grant was told by his doctor that he needed to take up a sport which would put him out of doors and give him fresh air and exercise. The doctor even suggested the game of golf. President Grant took some lessons, felt he was in condition to play a round of golf, and invited some friends to be with him.

On the first tee his friends insisted that he go first. He put the little white ball up on the little wooden tee and practiced a couple of swings. He was really going to show them what he could do. With a mighty swing he missed the ball. He stepped back again and took a couple more practice swings. This time he was really going to hit it.

For the second time the club head missed the ball. This time President Grant was embarrassed and turned a little red. He stepped back for more practice swings. This time he was going to knock it a country mile, but the wind from the club head caused the ball to roll off the tee. He was frustrated. He turned to his friends and said, "I never swear, but there are moments, and where I spit the grass will never grow again." All of us can find an appropriate response to moments of frustration and live that higher kind of law.

The Savior said, "Thou hast heard, an eye for an eye, and a tooth for a tooth"—the law of retribution. He gave them the higher law of turning the other cheek. "If they ask for your coat, give them your cloak also. If they ask you to go one mile, go the second mile." (Cf. Matthew 5:38-41.) This is a beautiful indication of how we should react to any situation in which we are asked to do something.

71

And the Lord said, "Thou hast heard, love thy friend but hate thine enemy. I say unto you, love thine enemy, bless them that curse you, do good to them that hate you, and pray for them that despitefully use you." (Cf. Matthew 5:43-44.)

In almost any of the commandments we can find a higher interpretation. For example, consider the last of the Ten Commandments — thou shalt not covet. I can imagine the Savior saying, "I'll give you, in this, the last dispensation, a higher law, so that you won't even think of coveting: the welfare plan. Be self-sufficient, live within your means, have a year's supply of food on hand." The welfare plan is a higher law than the tenth commandment.

A higher interpretation of "love thy father and thy mother" might be, "Also love thy forefathers and do thy genealogy work." Another interpretation might be, "Form an eternal family of thine own — eternal marriage in the temple." For almost any of the commandments, we can find a higher interpretation.

GO BEYOND OBEDIENCE

Let's examine the principle of obedience. We've all heard the parable of the father with the two sons. He said to the first, "Go to the vineyard and work." The first son said, "No," but then repented and went. The father said the same thing to the second son, who replied, "Yes," but then forgot or chose not to go. (Cf. Matthew 21:28-30.)

Now let's use the parable of the father with the five sons. All of the sons were asked to go to the vineyard to work. The first son said, "No." Rebellious, ornery, he didn't go. The second son said, "No," but then afterwards repented and went. The third son said, "Yes, I'll go," but then became distracted and didn't go. The fourth son said, "Yes," and he went. A great son, a wonderful son. He did a good job.

The fifth son, however, sought a higher interpretation of the law of obedience. Before the father got to him, he went to his father and said, "Dad, I've gone to the vineyard. I've pruned, weeded, fertilized, watered, fixed the fence and gate. I brought the tractor back and put it in the garage. Dad, what else can I do?" The fifth son understood the higher interpretation of the law of obedience — of not needing to be commanded in all things. He had initiative and resourcefulness.

I had an instructor in the navy, a fine man who had been a test pilot. One of his responsibilities was to test a fighter plane that was important to the factory. If they didn't sell it, they would go bankrupt. It was also important to the navy, which needed a quality aircraft to operate on aircraft carriers. In those days there were no electronic instruments aboard. He had to fly the aircraft, the prototype, and then tell the owners of the factory and the admirals whether it passed the test. They watched him take off and climb. After a long period of time he returned, landed, and climbed out of the aircraft.

All of the engineers, designers, owners, and admirals were there to hear him say, "As you saw, the aircraft jumped off the ground in less than the required distance." They all nodded. "Time to thirty thousand feet was so many minutes and so many seconds." Everybody ooed and ahhed. "It climbs like a homesick angel." Tremendous! "Speed at full throttle, straight and level, exceeded the calculations of the engineers by 14 percent." Everyone was impressed and the engineers were calculating how much that must have been. "On a power dive the wings didn't come off, nothing bent." But then he said, "It didn't pass the test. When I put it through the maneuvers which a fighter plane must be able to perform — when I tried to do the snap rolls, the loops, the evasive maneuvers — this aircraft would not respond to the controls. It was like a mule that gets the bit in its mouth and wants to go straight. Nothing I could do would make it turn fast enough. You'll have to make larger, more sensitive control surfaces so that the aircraft will be obedient to the pilot."

I've seen missionaries in the mission field who are very intelligent and have great talent and tremendous ability but fail because they aren't responsive to the controls. They aren't quite obedient. They don't understand that the rules are, first, to protect them from Satan and, second, to bless them with success. There are many interpretations, higher interpretations, of the law of obedience.

BECOME TRULY UNSELFISH

Consider the law of unselfishness. Let me use an interpretation of the parable of the prodigal son. You all know the story of the errant son who wasted away the inheritance he asked of his father. He came back tragically humbled. The father saw him from far off and loved him, hugged him, and sent the servants off to dress him with rings, robes, and shoes. He even declared a festival in his honor and killed the fatted calf. The older brother saw the party and asked what had happened. When he heard, he was upset and went to his father and said, "Lo, these many years do I serve thee, neither transgressed I at any time thy commandments: and yet thou never gavest me a [party] that I might make merry with my friends." (Luke 15:29.)

The father's explanation was not a rebuke, just a simple explanation. "Son, thou art ever with me, and all that I have is thine. . . . [But] this thy brother was dead, and is alive again; and was lost, and is found." (Luke 15:31-32.)

Imagine with me a higher interpretation of the story. I can now see the older son saying, "Father, forgive me. Wouldn't it be a good idea to divide my inheritance with

74

my brother who has returned?" Can't you see the increased joy of that father, who responds, "This, my other son that was lost in selfishness, is found again." I can see him calling the servants and saying, "Get my finest clothes, and my finest rings, and my finest shoes, and put them on this my elder son. Kill another fatted calf and call all of his friends, let us have a great party together. We who were lost to each other are found again."

SEEK TRUE PEACE

There is a higher interpretation of the principle of peace. The Savior is the Prince of Peace. Great interpretations have been given to that title. One of the finest I have ever heard was by President Harold B. Lee. President Joseph Fielding Smith had just died. President Lee was now the prophet. His first major meeting as the prophet was in Mexico at an area conference. In his first press conference as prophet, held there, he was asked a trap question.

"What is your position with regard to the Vietnam involvement — the Vietnam War?" It was a hot political issue at the time. If President Lee said, "I'm in favor of being there," the reporters would headline it, "How strange, a religious leader in favor of war." If President Lee said, "I'm against it," they would say, "How strange, a religious leader who pretends to support his government is against his own government."

It was a difficult question. President Lee's answer was inspired. It relied on a higher interpretation of the law. He said, "We, together with the entire Christian world, abhor war." Then he said, "The Savior, however, said that in the world there would be tribulations. He said, 'In me ye might have peace.' " (John 16:33.) President Lee went on to say, "The Savior said, 'Peace I leave with you, my peace I give unto you: not as the world giveth, give I unto you.' (John

75

14:27.) The Savior was not talking about the kind of peace that you can win with armies and bombs and rockets. He was talking about the kind of peace a person can have in his own heart, no matter what kind of tribulations there may be in the world." President Lee so won the understanding and sympathy of those worldly reporters that they gave good coverage to the conference and excellent coverage to him as a religious leader. From him they learned the higher interpretation.

THE WAY UP CAN BE THE WAY DOWN

There is another aspect of the higher law: The Lord's way is not always our way. The parable of the Pharisee and the publican illustrates this. The Savior observed two men who entered the temple to pray. The Pharisee said, "Thank God I'm not as other men are. I fast twice a week, and I tithe all I possess." Today he would have added, "I observe the Word of Wisdom, and I do my home teaching. Look what a great man I am. I'm thankful I'm not as other men are." The publican, the tax collector — very much looked down upon in those days — prayed, "God, be merciful to me a sinner." The Savior went on to say, "The publican, the second, is justified, rather than the Pharisee. For every one that exalteth himself shall be abased; and he that humbleth himself shall be exalted." (Cf. Luke 18:10-14.)

Allow me a personal interpretation. I fear there are too many self-righteous, holier-than-thou, better-than-thou in our ranks. I see too many who tend to look down upon other religions and other religious leaders. Some feel we have a particular corner on spirituality. We need to give more Christian love to those of other religions — more respect, more attention.

Although born and raised in the Church, I went to a Catholic university at the age of seventeen — straight from

BYU to Gonzaga University in Spokane, Washington. Every professor of mine was a Jesuit priest who wore the black full-length cassock. Every one held a Ph.D. And every one was a great Christian gentleman. I went there scared to death, the only Latter-day Saint boy on the entire campus. But they didn't ridicule my church, or me. I came to see them as spiritual leaders who were making tremendous sacrifices in their own lives.

In South America I saw many Protestant missionaries living in the jungles, doing a magnificent work, sacrificing themselves and their families — their entire lives. They don't have eighteen-month or even three-year missions — they are out there for a lifetime in the jungles. They are to be honored and respected for the work they do.

I had many Jewish clients in the years I was in international banking, and I never lost money on a loan to anyone of the Jewish faith. Every one of them paid.

In 1943, during World War II, the SS *Dorchester,* a troop ship, was torpedoed with nine hundred souls aboard in the north Atlantic in wintertime. It went down so fast that only two hundred and fifty or so survived. It was evident that not everyone was going to be able to get into the lifeboats. There were four chaplains on board: a Jewish rabbi, a Catholic priest, and two Protestant ministers. The survivors said the chaplains were seen helping others into the lifeboats. Then they were seen linking their arms together, the four of them bowing their heads in prayer, as the ship went under. There's a chapel in Philadelphia built in honor of those four chaplains. The motto of the chapel is "Unity without uniformity." That's a lofty spiritual goal for all of us.

The way up is down. King Benjamin said it beautifully. "If ye should serve him with all your whole souls yet ye would be unprofitable servants." (Mosiah 2:21.) Have a lively sense of your own guilt, Mosiah said. (See Mosiah 2:38.) Now, we don't need to have a lively guilt complex. If it's doing that to you, it's wrong. He goes on to say that a saint is meek and humble. Be aware of your own nothingness. "Remember . . . the greatness of God, and your own nothingness." (Mosiah 4:11.)

GET RID OF NEGATIVE FEELINGS

In order to climb up through the storms and the turbulence of life, it is necessary to lighten the load. Many of us have excess baggage consisting of guilt. In the process of repentance, confession is necessary. Get rid of jealousy. It is a poison to the spirit. Get rid of contention of any kind, usually caused by selfish pride—"I want it done my way." There is even a song about doing it my way. That doesn't get rid of contention. Get rid of rivalries, get rid of criticizing each other, get rid of negative thoughts, get rid of petty arguments.

Whenever we speak of rising above ourselves, rising to higher spiritual levels, there is a usual list of things to do. The *scriptures* certainly lift us to higher levels. *Prayer* is definitely a necessity for rising appropriately—not only traditional prayer, but frequent, heartfelt prayer with your eyes open while you are driving, or while you are walking and enjoying beautiful things. Talk to the Lord. Learn to pray with your eyes open. Learn also to serve others. Attend church, be worthy of a temple recommend, listen to beautiful spiritual music. Establish proper priorities. "Seek ye first the kingdom of God, and his righteousness." (Matthew 6:33.)

Try also to have the proper motivation. I see all too often out in the mission field an element of ambition. "I want to be the assistant to the president." I see it sometimes in those who say, "Gee, I'd like to be the first bishop in my family or the first stake president in my family." Misplaced ambition will never lift you to spiritual heights. The only ambition in the kingdom that does lift one up is to have "an eye single to the glory of God." (D&C 4:5.) In other words, if you're looking for the glory of the Lord, and you are working hard, then all things will be in place in appropriate ways.

UNDERSTAND THE COVENANTS

Also necessary for rising to a higher spiritual level are covenants — the covenants and the ordinances in which we enter into a contract with our Heavenly Father. There is a series of contracts that we don't speak very much about. I refer to temple covenants.

In D&C 52 we find instruction that I believe makes a beautiful statement about the temple. "I will give unto you a pattern in all things, that ye may not be deceived; for Satan is abroad in the land, and he goeth forth deceiving the nations." We are then told how to avoid Satan's deceptions. "He that prayeth, whose spirit is contrite, the same is accepted of me [and, I say, protected by the Lord against Satan] *if* he obey mine ordinances. He that speaketh, whose spirit is contrite, whose language is meek and edifieth, the same is of God [and, I'm adding, protected by God against the maneuvers of Satan] *if* he obey mine ordinances." The temple covenants are the highest ordinances of this dispensation. (D&C 52:14-16.)

I learned celestial navigation when I was in the navy, but true navigation, to me, is Hugh Nibley's kind of navigation. He says, "When I go to the temple, I can take my bearings on the universe." Understand the temple and what those ordinances can do to lift you above the trials and tribulations and the storms of life.

SEEK SUPERIOR FRIENDSHIPS

Let's look at the higher law of self-control. We're here in this life to learn self-control — control of our appetites and passions. To move higher, we need to associate with higher-minded friends. All of us enjoy friends who put up with us regardless of our weaknesses. On the other hand, do you have friends who are keeping you from achieving your goals? We must ask ourselves the question and then do what is necessary to seek loftier levels. What do our friends do with their spare time? What is their language level? What kind of movies do they attend? How do they spend their money? Ask yourself these questions about your friends. President Kimball says, "Seek superior friendships."

LOOK AHEAD

What about coping with tragedy? All of us will face difficult circumstances in life — the death of a loved one, illness, the loss of jobs, failure in ambitions and aspirations. Each of us should look ahead and prepare for tragedy or unexpected reverses by helping others who suffer. Learn from observing the strengths and weaknesses of others. Involvement in Christlike service to others builds a reserve — a sort of investment — so that we can face tragedy when we are called on to do so. Accept normal grief. All of us are going to lose some of those who are near and dear to us. Consolation comes through the Holy Ghost. Anytime we fight against what the Lord has seen fit to bring about, anytime we struggle against it, we will not be able to receive the blessings of the Holy Ghost — the consolation, the comfort, the understanding. We need that understanding of drawing nearer to our Savior and to our Heavenly Father.

The habit of happiness leads one to a higher spiritual level. Make a habit of happiness. Rise above an inferiority complex, learn to cope with failure. We're living in a society that praises winning so much that sometimes we haven't prepared those who aren't going to be the gold-, silver-, and bronze-medal winners. It was interesting to watch the Olympics on one occasion. The gold-medal winner in one event was, of course, enthusiastic. The silver-medal winner, second in the entire world, was in tears. The bronze-medal winner was ecstatic. She hadn't expected to be there. Our reactions are all relative to our expectations, so learn the habit of coping with temporary failure. Ralph Waldo Emerson said, "A man's success is made up of progressive failures which he rises above, because he experiments and ventures every day. And the more falls he gets, the faster he moves on." In Argentina the gauchos say, "You're never a good rider until you've been thrown a few times."

Consider this statement: "Wisdom comes from good judgment, good judgment comes from experience, experience comes from poor judgment." Think about that.

CHANGE TO A HIGHER LEVEL

There are higher laws of love. The telestial level is: "I have to do it," and you do it out of *fear*. The terrestrial level is: "I ought to do it," and you do it out of a sense of *duty*. The celestial level is: "I want to do it," and you do it because of *love*. President McKay said, "Man is a spiritual being, a soul. There is something within man which urges him to rise above himself, to control his environment, to master the body and all things physical, to live in a higher and a more beautiful world."

Wherever we are, we can find the way to live at a higher level. This will take us above the storms and the turbulence and the problems of life. We can soar with the eagles. We are of divine origin. We are children of our Heavenly Father. Our Heavenly Father lives and He loves us and He hears our prayers and He answers them. Jesus the Christ lives, and He loves us.

By Faith and Hope, All Things Are Fulfilled

ELDER PAUL H. DUNN

The Church Office Building stands twenty-six stories high. In it are two banks of elevators, one an express, one that moves a little more normally. One day I got on the express elevator. Some of the workers there say it could qualify as a ride at Disneyland. A little boy and his father got on with me. Suddenly the elevator took off, and the little boy, not expecting the thrill, lost his breath and looked up at his dad with great faith and trust and said, "Daddy, does Heavenly Father know we're coming?"

There is a great lesson in that experience.

Dr. JoAnn Larsen, a Salt Lake City family therapist, gave some wise and practical counsel on teaching children and building their self-esteem. She reminded us of the tendency most parents have, in their efforts to teach their children responsibility, of so often stressing the negative things the children do — the mistakes and misjudgments they make and the inconveniences and trouble they cause. She made the statement that between birth and twenty years of age the average child hears from parents, teachers, siblings, and peers some one hundred thousand negative messages, which are rarely balanced with positive messages. With an extremely lucky child, the ratio would probably be ten negatives to one positive, which she claims can be highly damaging, often for life, to a child's feelings of self-worth.

She encourages us all to develop lenses — vision that sees positives instead of negatives — thus making it possible to perform miracles sometimes and certainly to greatly improve the results of our teaching efforts and our parent-child relationships. The good accomplished toward the making of a better world through upbuilding, trusting approaches to life situations, in contrast to those that tear down, could very possibly never be accurately assessed.

Why is it that as humans we tend to emphasize the negative when there is so much to be positive about? We not only constantly criticize our children and each other, find fault, are very judgmental, and often seek out and build up people's weaknesses and failings rather than their strengths and successes, but in our own personal life-styles there are those of us who are incessant, chronic worriers. We worry about all the negative things that could happen, but usually don't, rather than positively trying to face problems with some amount of faith and hope of success.

In our society, for some reason, we seem to dwell on the bizarre, the tragic, the profane, and the evils of our day. So often the newspapers and television reports center attention around the negative aspects of life: teenage suicides, drugs, AIDS, murders, infidelities, dishonesty, and a host of other social ills.

As I travel throughout the Church, I occasionally see another form of thinking that can become quite negative — members weighted down, sometimes grimly, with the serious tasks they must perform to earn livings, pay mortgages, rear children, faithfully fulfill Church callings, attend to school and community responsibilities, live righteously and worthily — the list could go on and on.

I often think that for some of these people the joy and excitement have gone out of their lives and all they have to look back on are crowded, grim days, often filled with great guilt because of the pressure of trying to accomplish everything they think is necessary and to be perfect right now. Interestingly, negative attitudes seem to affect us in that way.

Now, of course, life is serious. Children must be taught, bills must be paid, we must live righteously — it is the Lord's counsel to us. We can't help but worry sometimes; there are and always will be never-ending negatives existing all around us which must be faced, dealt with, and solved. But I wonder if the constant bombardment of dilemmas and challenges and the often seemingly hopeless situations, both personal and nationwide, don't frustrate, discourage, and depress us sometimes to the point where our minds and attitudes are distracted from the very principles that would allow us to rise above the negative and find the positive answers we need.

In spite of the many negative occurrences in life, there are those who seem to have the knack of seeing the positive side. A young businessman was opening a new branch office, and a friend sent a floral arrangement to help celebrate the occasion. When the friend arrived at the opening, he was appalled to find that the wreath bore the inscription "Rest in Peace." Angry, he later complained to the florist. After apologizing, the florist said, "Look at it this way. Somewhere today a man was buried under a wreath that said, 'Good luck in your new location.' "

In the Book of Mormon, in which we find many answers and so much direction in solving problems, there is a scripture that, to me, sheds great light on the matter of a positive, trusting, hopeful attitude of faith as a substitute for facing life's problems with discouragement and despair. Listen to the words of the prophet Ether as he exhorts us to know and believe in God as a foundation of hope and faith:

"By faith all things are fulfilled—

"Wherefore, whoso believeth in God might with surety hope for a better world, yea, even a place at the right hand of God, which hope cometh of faith, maketh an anchor to the souls of men, which would make them sure and steadfast, always abounding in good works, being led to glorify God." (Ether 12:3-4.)

Throughout the whole of this marvelous chapter we are taught the wonders accomplished by faith, love, and hope. It seems to me that dwelling on negative thoughts and approaches is, in fact, working directly opposite of hope, faith, and trust—in the Lord, ourselves, and others—and causes continual feelings of gloom, while the positive lifts and buoys us up, encourages us to forge ahead, and is an attitude that can be developed, a habit that we can cultivate.

The epitome of celebrating the beautiful and overlooking the misfortune is the story of Thomas Moore.

Soon after he was married, Thomas Moore, the famous nineteenth-century Irish poet, was called away on a business trip. Upon his return he was met at the door, not by his beautiful bride, but by the family doctor.

"Your wife is upstairs," said the doctor. "But she asked that you not come up." Then Moore learned the terrible truth: his wife had contracted smallpox. The disease had left her once flawless skin pocked and scarred. She had taken one look at her reflection in the mirror and commanded that the shutters be drawn and that her husband never see her again. Moore would not listen. He ran upstairs and threw open the door of his wife's room. It was black as night inside. Not a sound came from the darkness. Groping along the wall, Moore felt for the gas jets.

A startled cry came from a black corner of the room. "No!" she said. "Don't light the lamps!"

Moore hesitated, swayed by the pleading in the voice.

"Go!" she begged. "Please go! This is the greatest gift I can give you now."

Moore did go. He went down to his study, where he sat up most of the night, prayerfully writing. Not a poem this time, but a song. He had never written a song before, but now he found it more natural to his mood than simple poetry. He not only wrote the words, but he wrote the music, too. The next morning, as soon as the sun was up, he returned to his wife's room.

He felt his way to a chair and sat down. "Are you awake?" he asked.

"I am," came a voice from the far side of the room. "But you must not ask to see me. You must not press me, Thomas."

"I will sing to you, then," he answered. And so for the first time, Thomas Moore sang to his wife the song that still lives today:

"Believe me, if all those endearing young charms which I gaze on so fondly today, were to change by tomorrow and flee in my arms like fairy gifts fading away, thou would'st still be adored, as this moment thou art — let thy loveliness fade as it will."

Moore heard a movement from the dark corner where his wife lay in her loneliness. He continued:

"Let thy loveliness fade as it will, and around the dear ruin each wish of my heart would entwine itself verdantly still —"

The song ended. As his voice trailed off on the last note, Moore heard his bride rise. She crossed the room to the window, reached up, and drew open the shutters.

We need more such attitudes in the world. There is the

story of the husband and wife who had saved and saved for a new car. After taking delivery, the husband told his wife that all the necessary legal documents and insurance information were in a packet in the glove compartment. On her first day out in the new car, she was involved in an accident, which demolished the front end of the car. Unhurt, in tears, and near panic, she opened the packet to show the police officer her papers. There she found a handwritten note from her husband which read: "Now that you have had an accident, remember I can always replace the car, but not you. Please know how much I love you!"

As stated in the beginning that with children we so often see the negative before the positive, a little boy was almost squelched in his attempt to express his feelings because an adult didn't understand. A special friend of mine, Dr. Thomas Myers, shared this tender experience:

A small boy accompanied his father and grandparents into his medical office. The old man was leaning on the boy's two outstretched hands as he moved. The child encouraged him with, "Come on, Grandpa, you can make it! . . . Only a little farther, Grandpa. . . . The doctor will make your leg better." A sweet grandmother walked behind.

After the visit, the three exited the same way. The little boy was given a helium balloon on his way out. He helped his grandfather to the car, then ran back in and, pulling himself up to the counter, asked the receptionist, "Please, may I have another balloon?"

His grandmother, still standing there, scolded him, "Of course you can't. I warned you not to let that balloon go!" She apologized to the receptionist. "He did this last week — went right outside and let his balloon go. I really did warn him this time."

The little boy was trying to tell her something. She bent down to listen. Then, with tears showing on her thin, wrinkled face, the grandmother asked, "Could he please have another balloon? You see, his little sister died a few months ago, and he wanted her to have a balloon to play with, too!"

As critical and judgmental as we often must be, as much as we will have to correct, as truly as we must face unpleasant realities all of our days, let us recognize and praise the thousands of beauties of life around us; the many wonderful examples of virtuous living; the strengths and the courage of so many souls; the exceptional talents and achievements of our family members, neighbors, and associates; the countless blessings that we have been given. As has been quoted by so many, but seems to fit so well here, "Two men look out through the same bars: One sees mud, and one the stars." (Frederick Langbridge, *A Cluster of Quiet Thoughts*, cited in *The Oxford Dictionary of Quotations*, 2d ed., London: Oxford University Press, 1966, p. 310.)

And as the prophet Mormon taught us:

"But charity [in this case, the charity in our thoughts about and appreciation of others] is the pure love of Christ, and it endureth forever; and whoso is found possessed of it at the last day, it shall be well with him." (Moroni 7:47.)

Remember, Christ came to lift us up, not put us down.

TRUST IN THE LORD

ELDER GENE R. COOK

Some years ago a young man I'll call Raymond was in the seventh grade. He was a little taller than the other boys and did quite well in basketball and track. But as the year progressed, the basketball coach began saying to him, "Raymond, stay seated. You're no ball player. You're too clumsy." The next game, "No, we don't need you. You stay right there. You can't run. You can't shoot the ball. You're not fast enough." This process continued for a number of months.

The inevitable happened. Because of that continual negative conditioning, Raymond finally believed what he was being told about himself. He bought it hook, line, and sinker. He believed it so much that in coming years he did his best to avoid the gym altogether. He did not play basketball with the young men at Church or at school. He stopped running. He avoided sports and went through high school minimizing interaction of any kind in sports. The negative conditioning even followed him into his first year of college. Again he minimized his involvement to the smallest degree possible.

A year later he found himself on a mission in a distant land. In this particular country the buses did not stop to let people on or off. Passengers had to learn to do that on the run.

One afternoon Raymond and his companion were a block from the bus stop when they saw the bus coming. One of them said, "Run, Elder, run, or we'll miss our next appointment." To Raymond's great surprise, he beat his companion to the bus stop. That afternoon Raymond purposely arranged more runs for the bus. Each time he beat his companion.

He was shocked and amazed. He knew his companion had received a number of awards for being the fastest runner in all of northern Arizona.

It was then that Raymond suddenly realized that he'd wasted all those years. He could have excelled in athletics, but he had believed what someone else had sown in his mind.

Have you ever done that? Has someone convinced you that you are not good at music or mathematics or that you'll always be overweight? Each of us definitely received different gifts. But I am convinced that many of us are severely limited by the beliefs we have about ourselves.

Solomon said, "For as [a man] thinketh in his heart, so is he." (Proverbs 23:7.) And the Lord said, "And then, behold, according to your desires, yea, even according to your faith shall it be done unto you." (D&C 11:17.) You cannot rise higher than your own beliefs and thoughts about yourself. Jesus said, "If thou canst believe, *all things are possible to him that believeth.*" (Mark 9:23; emphasis added.)

One of the great processes you go through in life is to discover yourself, to find those gifts and capacities God has given you. He has given you great talents, the smallest part of which you have just begun to utilize. Trust the Lord to assist you in unlocking the door to those gifts. Some of us have created imaginary limits in our minds. There is literally a genius locked up inside each of us. Don't ever let anyone convince you otherwise.

May I tell you about an experience another young man faced? He was eighteen years of age, and I'll call him Raymond also. This young man found himself in a speech class at a university. He had received a scholarship and was anxious to maintain a good grade point average. For that reason his heart sank when, one day, the instructor announced, "Students, you will be pleased to know that in the last twenty-five years of teaching I've only given five A's."

Raymond tried to transfer from the class but was unable to do so. Through the months he received B's, B-'s, and once in a while, a B+, but never an A. He was disheartened. Thirty days from the conclusion of the term the teacher stood up and said to the class, "You each have one last talk to give. It will determine half of your grade. You must select an extremely controversial subject, talk for twenty-five minutes, make an actual defense of the subject the best you can, be prepared to receive a purposeful attack upon you and your subject after you have finished, and receive a written critique afterwards from each student in the class."

A great hush came over the class, mostly prompted by self-doubt and fear. Some thought of talking on communism versus democracy, racial issues, birth control—anything that would be controversial.

Numbers were drawn to determine who would speak first. Raymond drew number nine. As the days went by and he saw the grueling experience each speaker went through, fear mounted in his heart about what he should do.

He prayed about a topic, but he could not seem to settle on anything. It was now just two days until he was to give his speech, and he had nothing in writing. Yet one impression seemed to recur to him: "If you're looking for a controversial subject, choose the Book of Mormon. That's controversial enough."

Raymond was fearful, however, because he knew he was the only member of the Church in the class. He also knew that the teacher was an active member of a Protestant church. Throughout the entire semester as she taught passages from the Bible, she had made it clear that she regarded the Bible as the only revelation from God to man.

Raymond struggled with himself. He feared the whole idea might backfire. But he finally decided to do it. He had served a stake mission the previous summer and knew the missionary lesson depicting the Bible and Book of Mormon as scripture to the old and new worlds.

The day of his presentation he announced his subject as the Book of Mormon. A hush fell over the class. He began teaching with an academic approach, hoping to not offend. But about halfway through, the Spirit of the Lord came upon him and he thought to himself, "I can't just tell them historically about this book. I don't care what they think of me, or what happens to my grade. These folks are going to get it. The Book of Mormon is true. They ought to all know it."

From that point on he taught the lesson much as it was written to be given to investigators, bearing his testimony frequently. He even concluded in the name of Jesus Christ and said amen.

He then waited for the attack. To his astonishment, not a word was spoken by the students. The teacher tried to prompt them to attack. They would not. Not one word was spoken. Finally, in frustration, the teacher said, "Be seated, Raymond."

The written student reviews were all positive. Four or five wrote, "You have almost convinced me of the truth of what you have spoken." One individual who was particularly critical of the other students' presentations wrote, "I really would like to know more about your church."

What great faith it took for this young man to proceed and to teach what he knew was right in the face of almost sure ridicule. To his delight, Raymond received an A in that class. The Lord truly blesses any one of us that keeps the commandments and is not afraid to bear witness of Him as He has commanded all of us "to stand as witnesses of God at all times and in all things, and in all places that ye may be in." (Mosiah 18:9.)

Didn't Paul speak with the Spirit, saying, "For I am not ashamed of the gospel of Christ: for it is the power of God unto salvation to every one that believeth." (Romans 1:16.)

"Trust in the Lord with all thine heart; and lean not unto thine own understanding. In all thy ways acknowledge him, and he shall direct thy paths." (Proverbs 3:5-6.)

Remember, "To be learned is good if they hearken unto the counsels of God." (2 Nephi 2:29.)

You may have faced, or you will face, the world just as this young man did. How much faith will you have? Never be embarrassed of the gospel, but go forward and testify of that which you believe.

Don't act as a novice pretending to know it all. One novice, a tourist from the East camping in the mountains of the West, humorously said to a seasoned guide, "Is it true that a grizzly bear won't attack you if you're carrying a lantern?" The man thought a moment and said, "Well, Sonny, it depends on how fast you're carrying it!"

Some of us, in making decisions, lay out plans like the tourist in the forest, or like another tourist who followed the counsel for a surefire way to catch a porcupine: Get up in a tree with a large steel tub. When the porcupine comes by, drop the tub over the porcupine. This provides something to sit on while planning the next move.

We can surely do better than that in doing our planning of life's critical decisions.

Let me tell about another young man whom I'll also call Raymond.

When he was eleven, Raymond obtained a paper route and began to prosper. At age sixteen he was still delivering papers. One day the manager of the newspaper came in and said, "Raymond, you have been so loyal and done so well in selling subscriptions that I'm going to appoint you assistant manager of circulation of this newspaper. In your duties you'll supervise the other paper boys and teach them how to sell subscriptions. After school, after finishing your route, you'll be able to come to the office to work two or three hours. You'll be able to do some homework while you're waiting to answer complaints on the phone. All in all, it will be a great job for you. And by the way, your pay will be tripled."

Raymond was delighted. He wanted to go on a mission and was saving money for that day. This job would simply accelerate the process. He counted his blessings. This seemed to be the ideal job, and at a time when many teenagers had no work.

Repeatedly he said to himself, "My, the Lord blesses one who keeps the commandments." He had always paid his tithing, kept the Sabbath day holy, and honored his priesthood. He also felt he was being blessed for resisting the pressure to study on Sunday.

A year and a half went by. One Saturday, George, the newspaper manager, came to him and said, "One week from now we're going to begin delivering the Sunday paper. You will not only have your Sunday route to deliver early in the morning, but you'll have to stay in the office from about 7:00 A.M. to 2:00 P.M. You'll also receive a 30 percent increase in pay."

The manager quickly added, "I know you're a Mormon, and you may be thinking of not taking this extra job beyond your route. If you don't take the job, you'll not only lose the opportunity to earn more money on Sunday, but you'll also lose your paper route and be fired from your weekday job as well. There are many of my other paper boys who would give their right arm to have your job."

Raymond was despondent. He prayed over and over, "How could this be, Heavenly Father? I have kept the commandments. I've tried to do what is right. I'm trying to go on a mission. Now I may lose my job. Shall I work this added job on Sunday, or not?"

He emotionally explained the problem to his father, who replied, "I don't know the answer, but I know someone who does," meaning the Lord.

Raymond struggled with the problem. He talked to his bishop. He learned that, if he decided to work, there were sacrament meetings being held in other wards in the afternoon that he could attend. He prayed and struggled with the problem two full days.

Tuesday, when George asked for his decision, Raymond said with great emotion, "I love my job and my route, but I cannot work on Sunday."

George responded emphatically, "You're fired! Come in Saturday to pick up your last check. There are many young men who would be glad to have a job like this. You're an ungrateful young man!" Then he stomped out of the office.

The next three or four days were hard for Raymond. The manager scarcely spoke to him. He wondered if he had made the right decision. He thought to himself, "There are many who have to work on Sunday because of their employment. Shouldn't I?" But the answer seemed to be the same: "There may be some who have to work on Sunday, but you don't have to and should not."

Saturday morning finally arrived, and Raymond went in to pick up his last check. As he walked into the office, George grabbed him by the arm and took him to a nearby room. "Raymond, please forgive me. I was wrong. I ought not to have tried to make you break the commandments. I have found another young man who is willing to do the extra work on Sunday. You can keep your job. Will you?"

When Raymond agreed, the manager added, "You'll find the extra 30 percent I was going to pay you for the extra work on Sunday included in your paycheck this week, and also in your future paychecks, as long as you continue working for me."

What great joy Raymond felt as he went home that afternoon! Again and again he said to himself, "It is worth it to keep the commandments of the Lord. The Lord will always provide for his own." What joy Raymond felt a year later to see his manager in the congregation when he spoke preparatory to leaving for his mission.

What greater joy, twenty-six years later, for Raymond to find that George was active, faithful, and strong in the Church.

The Lord commanded us to "seek ye a living like unto men." (D&C 54:9.) But we are also commanded to be in the world but not be of it. Be careful that you never compromise the principles you believe in. Always trust in the Lord.

Let me tell you about another young man. We'll also call him Raymond.

Raymond became very ill while serving a mission in a distant land. Because of these health problems, the mission president considered sending him home. To compound Raymond's problems, one day he began having a severe pain in his left foot. He couldn't even walk to the discussion he and his companion had scheduled. They went instead to the doctor, who said, "It's just arthritis caused by the damp weather. If you'll stay off your foot for two or three days, the pain will pass."

Raymond did so. He also received a priesthood blessing. But nothing happened. He was a district leader at the time, and his district had just begun to baptize in a city where there had not been baptisms for some time. He could not understand how the Lord could allow him to remain down when his district was just beginning to have success.

A week went by, then two weeks, then a month. There was no change in the pain in his foot. Finally, he was taken to the mission home in the capital city where more suitable medical facilities were available.

There he learned that one of the bones in his foot had been fractured and had then grown back together incorrectly. The doctors talked of either breaking the bone again or giving him electrical treatments to fuse the bone correctly, but it would take another month. He was down again, going for treatments twice a day. The treatments didn't make any difference. This problem, on top of his other medical problems, had him discouraged, and again the consideration came to send him home.

One morning, after nearly three months, Raymond stepped out of bed to find absolutely no pain in his foot. He stepped on the foot gently, then stamped on it, then ran a mile with his companion that morning. He was totally healed and he returned immediately to work.

Two weeks later a letter arrived from home. It began, "Dear son," and then a paragraph of chastisement followed for not having told his family about his ailments in the mission field. They had learned of his problems from another missionary, a friend of his, who had written home. "As a family we have begun a fast and constant prayer for you.

We also have placed your name on the temple prayer list and hope that it might be of help to you."

As Raymond read the letter and referred to his journal, he found that the day he had risen from his bed was the day the letter had been written, the day his family had begun praying and exercising faith for him.

The reality of the power of faith cannot be denied. Remember the counsel — trust in the Lord.

Life is challenging. Major decisions face us all. But if we rely on the Lord, we will handle them successfully.

We see in all of these examples individuals who have acted in faith and have trusted in the Lord. The Lord really is the answer to our challenges, our problems, our future.

The following are a few suggestions that may help you stay close to and trust in the Lord:

1. Pray to him, continually seeking revelation throughout the day. (See 2 Nephi 9:52.)

2. Read the scriptures daily, even if for only a few minutes. They will teach you of the world to come and give you direction in this world. (See Helaman 3:27-30.)

3. Exercise faith, keep the things of the Spirit as the first priority in your life. All else will be appropriately added. (See Jacob 2:18.)

4. Seek to do His will — not your own — humbling yourself and repenting or changing your life as needed. (See Helaman 10:45.)

5. Love others, serve them, feed the Lord's flock. (See John 21:15-17.)

6. Keep the commandments with exactness. (See Alma 57:21.)

The Lord prospers those who keep His commandments. He said: "And if it so be that the children of men keep the commandments of God he doth nourish them, and strengthen them, and provide means whereby they can accomplish the thing which he has commanded them." (1 Nephi 17:3.)

If you will keep the commandments, He will nourish you, strengthen you, and provide the means for accomplishing all things necessary to faithfully finish your divine mission here on earth.

The four stories related in this chapter were actual occurrences in the life of Gene Raymond Cook.

THE FUTILITY OF FEAR

ELDER DEREK A. CUTHBERT

Anciently the Lord spoke to Isaac, saying, "Fear not, for I am with thee." (Genesis 26:24.) The admonition to "fear not" was clear and direct and meaningful. The promise that "I am with thee" was equally plain and powerful.

Down through the ages the same admonition, the same assurance, has been extended to every living soul who is willing to qualify. And yet fear is prevalent throughout the earth. It stifles initiative, saps strength, and reduces efficiency. It weakens faith, brings doubts, and begets mistrust. Indeed, it tends to impede the very business of being. How negative, frustrating, and futile is fear!

Let us consider then the futility of fear so that we may, as much as possible, overcome it and exclude it from our lives. Then will our efforts yield their full potential, and our minds will be unshackled and enlightened with eternal truth. One of the four essential human freedoms listed by Franklin D. Roosevelt in a message delivered to Congress on January 6, 1941, was "Freedom from Fear." Emily Bronte's immortal words are apt:

No coward soul is mine,
No trembler in the world's storm-troubled sphere:

100

I see Heaven's glories shine,
And faith shines equal, arming me from fear.
(*Last Lines*, 1846.)

How shall we then arm ourselves from fear?

Fear comes in all shapes and sizes. There are those who fear people; others fear things. Many fear the future, and some fear the past. Where do you fit in? I will present ten aspects of the futility of fear, and I trust that this sharing will be beneficial, uplifting, and arming.

First, there is fear of God. Among all of the possible fears, this is the only one that is valid. However, it is not fear in the normal sense of lack of courage, but rather love, respect, and reverence. Indeed, fear of God in this sense can dispel all other fears. Consider the assurance and admonitions given to the Israelites: "The Lord is with us: fear them not." (Numbers 14:9.) Paul issued the rhetorical question, "If God be for us, who can be against us?" (Romans 8:31), meaning, "who can prevail against us?" (JST Romans 8:31.)

Fear, or love, of God also brings many other blessings in addition to courage. "It shall be well with them that fear God" (Ecclesiastes 8:12), for He is "gracious unto those who fear" Him (D&C 76:5). Yes, fear, or love, of God releases us, frees us, just as acceptance of truth does, for "the truth shall make [us] free." (John 8:32.)

Second, there is fear of man. There are those who fear physical domination by others. The Psalmist gave good counsel that we should "not fear what flesh can do unto [us]." (Psalm 56:4.) Experience teaches that it is futile to be afraid, for fear attracts the attention of the bully and the derision of those who mock.

The Lord, through Moses, declared with firmness to the Israelites: "When thou goest out to battle against thine enemies, and seest horses, and chariots, and a people more than thou, be not afraid of them: for the Lord thy God is with thee, which brought thee up out of the land of Egypt." (Deuteronomy 20:1.)

To return good for evil not only overcomes fear but also overcomes enmity. I remember an unfriendly neighbor some years ago. He would play the radio very loudly and generally try to be objectionable — so much as to generate fear. I am glad I was prompted to retain a positive, cheerful demeanor that overcame fear and eventually broke down the barrier, for "perfect love casteth out fear." (1 John 4:18.)

Third. Much more prevalent than physical fear is the fear of criticism, rejection, and verbal opposition. The scriptures are replete with counsel and admonition. In latter-day revelation to Joseph Smith, the Lord said, in relation to the loss of 116 pages of manuscript of the Book of Mormon, "You should not have feared man more than God." (D&C 3:7.)

Saul was rejected as king because, as he confessed to Samuel, "I feared the people, and obeyed their voice." (1 Samuel 15:24.) Will you transgress the commandments of the Lord because you fear what others will say if you don't follow them in the ways of the world? "Fear ye not the reproach of men," the Lord counseled through Isaiah. (Isaiah 51:7.) In more recent times He has chided those who "will not open their mouths [to share the gospel] . . . because of the fear of man." (D&C 60:2.)

When we have something to tell others that will benefit them, protect them, or enlighten them, we should not hold back. There are so many people who are confused and discouraged and who want a better way of life. How grateful they are when someone takes the time to share their happiness and purpose in life! Will you seek to share even more? You are a great power for good, providing your righteous potential is harnessed by service.

While I served as mission president in Scotland from 1975 to 1978, the Church received considerable opposition and criticism. On one occasion, three ministers made derogatory public statements in a particular city. I wrote an open letter to the local newspaper announcing that we would be holding a public meeting in that city to dispel some of the misunderstandings which were being voiced around. It was a wonderful meeting. We first showed the fine Church film *Meet the Mormons,* and then I spoke to the large group concerning our beliefs and way of life. When we opened the meeting for questions, a number of people who were not members of the Church stood and said kind things about the Church and about Latter-day Saints they knew. Positive results ensued, and the work moved forward.

What if we had feared the criticism? I remember receiving a telephone call from a missionary who was obviously a little fearful. He said, "President, what shall we do? We have a man from the local church who follows us wherever we go and tries to stop us from knocking on the doors."

The young missionary was surprised at my response. "Good," I said. "You will have much success there, for the adversary is getting worried." I told him of the experience of the early missionaries to the British Isles just before the first baptisms took place in Preston. Elder Heber C. Kimball, grandfather of President Spencer W. Kimball, recorded it as follows: "By this time the adversary of souls began to rage, and he felt determined to destroy us before we had fully established the kingdom of God in that land, and the next morning I witnessed a scene of satanic power and influence which I shall never forget." (Orson F. Whitney, *Life of Heber C. Kimball,* Salt Lake City: Juvenile Instructor Office, 1888, p. 143.)

After my wife and I were baptized in January 1951, many of our neighbors shunned us, sometimes crossing the street so they would not meet us face to face. This did not affect our attitude, however, and we greeted them normally. It was not long before they began coming to us and asking, "We have a child who is ill, would you pray for her?" or "I have a problem. Would you please give me some counsel and advice?"

There is never any need to fear opposition, criticism, or persecution, for we know what will be the outcome. The Lord's work goes forward even more strongly. "The works, and the designs, and the purposes of God cannot be frustrated, neither can they come to naught. Remember, remember that it is not the work of God that is frustrated, but the work of men." (D&C 3:1, 3.)

Fourth. There are some who fear events, such as examinations and tests, interviews and journeys. These are all challenges that we need to shoulder. Fear usually brings failure. The Savior warned of "men's hearts failing them for fear." (Luke 21:26.) Eleanor Roosevelt said, "You gain strength, courage and confidence by every experience in which you really stop to look fear in the face." (*You Learn by Living*, 1960, as cited in John Bartlett, *Familiar Quotations*, Boston: Little, Brown and Company, 1968, p. 981.)

There is an excellent example of this when Elisha's servant discovered that the Syrian army had surrounded the city of Dothan, wherein they dwelt. Fearfully, he said to the prophet, "Alas, my master! how shall we do?"

Elisha answered him firmly: "Fear not: for they that be with us are more than they that be with them." (2 Kings 6:15-16.) Well could he say this, for "behold, the mountain was full of horses and chariots of fire round about Elisha." (2 Kings 6:17.)

One lesson we have to learn is that fear is the beginning

of defeat. On the other hand, courage is the beginning of success. We gain courage by the realization that we have a lot going for us. We derive strength from the knowledge that the Lord is with us. To Abraham he declared, "Fear not, Abram: I am thy shield." (Genesis 15:1.) This is exactly what we need in this tempting, permissive world — a shield to protect us from the "fiery darts of the wicked." (D&C 27:17.)

One great event that some people fear is referred to as "the end of the world." We know that at the second coming of Jesus Christ it will be the "great and dreadful day of the Lord" (Malachi 4:5, D&C 110:14) — *dread* being a synonym for fear. We can make it a great day for us, though, rather than a dreadful day. How? By qualifying, by complying, by following the Lord. It is futile to be afraid when we could be "looking forth for the great day of the Lord." (D&C 45:39.)

As a young boy, not quite thirteen years of age, in September 1939, it was natural to have some fear when I heard that war had been declared. During the dark days that followed, when the invasion of England seemed imminent and bombs were falling all around, some of the children even speculated about the end of the world coming. We were not really afraid, however, for we had faith in God. We prayed and worked for deliverance, and miraculously it came.

Another futile fear that I dispelled some years later was the fear of heights. We were building our new chapel in Nottingham, England, with all the members helping. My specialty was laying floor tile and placing ceiling tile in the corridors and classrooms. There was a call for someone to fix some ceiling tiles at the very apex of the chapel ceiling. As I started to climb the ladder, it seemed as though I was scaling Mount Everest. On reaching the top I had to measure exactly, then descend the ladder, cut the tiles to shape and size, climb it once again, and fit them in place. Certainly, the best way to overcome fear of heights is to "do it," as President Spencer W. Kimball challenged us. In fact, he said, "Give me another mountain."

Fifth. Another event which strikes fear and apprehension into the hearts of many is death. The prophet Mormon speaks of "that awful fear of death which fills the breasts of all the wicked." (Mormon 6:7.) This particular fear arises from misunderstanding the purpose of life and a lack of knowledge of the plan of our Father. It is vital to come to an understanding that death is not the end but a new beginning, a necessary stage in our eternal progression. Fear of death accomplishes nothing if we are righteous, for "death is swallowed up in victory . . . victory through our Lord Jesus Christ." (1 Corinthians 15:54, 57.)

David gave us magnificent words of comfort: "Yea, though I walk through the valley of the shadow of death, I will fear no evil: for thou art with me; thy rod and thy staff they comfort me." (Psalm 23:4.) Speaking of death in this way gives the Lord's perspective, whereas talking fearfully of death creates fear and uneasiness.

Some years ago, a dear young friend of ours, Pat, was stricken with cancer. She was not afraid of death, but she was concerned about her small children. She did not want to leave them while they were so young. Her great faith and courage were rewarded and she was granted a few vital years to care for her family before she peacefully passed away.

I think also of Joan, a very close friend, who was tragically killed by a car as she crossed a street in Salt Lake City. She certainly did not fear death, for she was fully prepared. Everything was in order in her personal life and in her personal papers. She was ready to meet the Lord.

Sixth, there are fears of the unknown. These may be experienced in a number of ways: fear of the dark, fear of change, fear of the future. Such fear can be overcome by faith, as the Lord showed as He rebuked the winds and the sea. "Why are ye fearful, O ye of little faith?" He challenged His disciples. (Matthew 8:26.)

The Lord's disciples succumbed to this type of fear on several occasions. When they saw Jesus walking on the water, He comforted them, saying, "Be of good cheer; it is I; be not afraid." (Matthew 14:27.) Again, when He appeared to them after His resurrection, they were "terrified and affrighted, and supposed that they had seen a spirit." He developed faith within them as He asked them to "handle me, and see; for a spirit hath not flesh and bones, as ye see me have." (Luke 24:37, 39.)

Reassurance from others is an important step towards faith. For example, there is the comfort given by parents to children afraid of the dark, or by a wife to a husband about to change his place of work. During my Royal Air Force service in India and Burma during World War II, one of our colleagues was always imagining a twisted stick to be a snake. We had to reassure him on numerous occasions to allay his fears. As Theseus remarked in Shakespeare's *A Midsummer Night's Dream:* "Or in the night, imagining some fear,/ How easy is a bush suppos'd a bear!" (Act 5, scene 1, lines 21-22.)

Again, concerning the future, is it unknown? The Lord has told us much about the future through His prophets. "Fear not," He has counseled, "let your hearts be comforted." (D&C 98:1.) "If ye are prepared ye shall not fear." (D&C 38:30.)

The pattern of the scriptures is first a commandment, then a promise. Providing we live our lives in harmony with the commandments of God, there is no place for fear regarding the consequences. "Seek ye first the kingdom of God, and his righteousness; and all these things shall be added unto you." (Matthew 6:33.) I have a strong testimony of this. For while we have not sought for worldly possessions, since we put our hands to the gospel plow, we have always had sufficient for our needs.

Seventh, we have fear of responsibility. Just after I joined the Church, a great feeling of confidence came over me. I felt that I had chosen the Lord's side, that He was on my side. Several remarkable things happened, of which I will recount but two.

Although I had never had the courage to stand on my feet and speak in debate, either at high school or college, I found myself asking my branch president if I might give a talk in sacrament meeting. I still have the notes of that very first talk. It was on faith and works.

A few months after my baptism, an opportunity presented itself at my place of work, where I was a management trainee. Again I had that strong feeling of self-assurance, and I received my first promotion, which set my feet on the management ladder. I found that through my Church membership and the faith it engendered, I overcame the fear of taking responsibility.

I have always loved reading Paul's epistles to Timothy. In particular I cherish this advice: "For God hath not given us the spirit of fear; but of power, and of love, and of a sound mind." (2 Timothy 1:7.) I have learned to rely on the Comforter, even the Holy Ghost, to give me the feeling of peace and confidence and to bring things to my remembrance.

Said the Savior: "Whosoever belongeth to my church need not fear." (D&C 10:55.) How true that is, for in His Church the gift of the Holy Ghost is available to all. We can be prompted about impending danger, as I have been on several occasions. We can discern places we should not go and things we should not do. It is futile to fear when the Holy Ghost is with you and the Lord himself is "on your right hand and on your left." (D&C 84:88.)

What of marriage responsibility? Are there some who delay marriage for fear of the responsibility? When my wife and I were married, we had between us the magnificent sum of twenty English pounds. Although young, we felt ready for the challenges and responsibilities ahead. What a glorious experience it has been for forty years to shoulder responsibility and struggle together in building a happy home and rearing a wonderful family of ten precious children!

From time to time I meet members of the Church who do not feel able to take responsibility as an officer or a teacher in the Church. I tell them of my experience in England. Within days of baptism I was called to head the youth program in the Nottingham Branch. This was completely new to me and I felt inadequate, but I knew the Lord needed me. There were less than seven thousand members in the whole of the British Isles where there are now forty stakes. We all had to be "anxiously engaged" in the work of saving souls, building the kingdom, and establishing Zion. So it is with all of us. It is futile to fear responsibility when we have been called to serve "by prophecy, and by the laying on of hands by those who are in authority." (Articles of Faith 1:5.)

Eighth is the fear of loneliness. Linked with this is the fear of being in a small minority. This type of fear often results in compromise of principles and giving in to the demands of others for fear of being lonely or being the odd one out. In latter-day revelation, the Lord has given comfort and assurance to those in this situation: "Fear not, little flock; do good; let earth and hell combine against you, for if ye are built upon my rock, they cannot prevail." (D&C 6:34.)

Fear of loneliness includes fear of not having anyone to talk to, or of being without help in time of need. These fears can be conquered by reaching out and giving service to others, becoming outward-looking instead of inward-looking. In order to have a friend, we must be a friend.

I think of Sister Amy Gent, whom I was privileged to visit for fifteen years as a branch president, home teacher, and friend. The first time I visited her, she was eighty-seven years of age. I was later honored to speak at the funeral of this wonderful lady who stepped from this life at age 102. Widowed twice, she was the only member of the Church in her extended family. Was she lonely? Never.

She read the scriptures every day and once asked me to take her some missionary tracts, which I assumed were to vary her reading. I gave them to her, saying, "You will enjoy reading these, Sister Gent."

"Oh, they are not for me," she replied. "I visit an old lady and I want to share the gospel with her."

Reaching out, helping, serving—this is the way to overcome the fear of loneliness.

A few weeks ago, a brother complained to me, "When I was away on business recently, in another part of the country, I went to church and no one spoke to me. I felt very lonely, especially as I was so far from home."

I paused and then asked, "How many people did you speak to?" At first he was a little annoyed, feeling I had not empathized, but then he smiled and said, "You're right, I did hold back instead of reaching out."

Ninth. Fear of the past haunts those who have transgressed and have not yet gained forgiveness and remission. President Kimball counseled: "To cure spiritual diseases which throttle us and plague our lives, the Lord has given us a sure cure—repentance." (*The Miracle of Forgiveness*, Salt Lake City: Bookcraft, 1969, preface.)

Furthermore, the Lord has given us a wonderful formula to enable us to remove fear and guilt: "Behold, he who has repented of his sins, the same is forgiven, and I, the Lord, remember them no more. By this ye may know if a man repenteth of his sins—behold, he will confess them and forsake them." (D&C 58:42-43.)

Confession is the first major step in the process of repentance. What a tremendous burden is lifted, which otherwise would weigh us down interminably. But sincere repentance is multifaceted; it is more than confession. There must be a forsaking and turning away from transgression in all its sordid forms.

Then we can look forward to and, indeed, claim fulfillment of the promise of the Lord—that He will not only forgive but remember our sins no more. What a contrast to the lot of those of whom Isaiah speaks: "Woe unto them that seek deep to hide their counsel from the Lord, and their works are in the dark, and they say, Who seeth us? and who knoweth us?" (Isaiah 29:15.)

On a number of occasions I have had the happy assignment to meet with those who have prepared to come back and once again embrace the gospel. What a great day it is for them! Fear of the past has fled and they begin anew.

We need to do some spring cleaning in our lives, to sweep out each nook and cranny. In the world of industry and commerce, regular inventory is taken. At these times, decisions are made to eliminate certain items from the inventory and to mark other items down in value. Taking inventory is a critical and necessary function.

We should take inventory in our lives, as did Scrooge,

and cast out the dross so that we become unencumbered and free from fear of the past.

When recommendations are being considered for appointment to public office, investigation of the personal life and affairs of the nominee is becoming more frequent. Whether we have aspirations for success in political, business, academic, or other spheres of activity, we should endeavor to keep ourselves "unspotted from the world." (James 1:27.) In order not to fear the past, try not to do anything in the present that you will regret or have to correct in the future.

Tenth, and finally, there is fear of failure. There are those who do not even attempt to do something because they lack the self-assurance that they can accomplish it. I was raised with the old adage ringing in my ears, "If at first you don't succeed, try, try again." There is no disgrace in failure; in any case, we have never failed until we give up. The four-minute mile eluded athletes for years, but after trying again and again, Roger Bannister finally achieved it. Since then, athletes from many lands have broken this barrier.

President N. Eldon Tanner remarked on one occasion, "One of the evils of the world today is not failure, but low aim." Just as we should not fear to fail, neither should we fear to aim high. There was no question of failure in the mind of Joseph Smith, the Prophet, when, in the dark days of 1842, he penned the words, "Brethren, shall we not go on in so great a cause? Go forward and not backward. Courage, brethren; and on, on to the victory!" (D&C 128:22.)

I say to you: Take courage. These are great times and there are great things to be accomplished. Develop your talents; do not hide them under a bushel. Prepare prayerfully and increase in faith, and you will never have need to fear. I declare with the poet, Longfellow:

> Our hearts, our hopes, are all with thee,
> Our hearts, our hopes, our prayers, our tears,
> Our faith triumphant o'er our fears,
> Are all with thee — are all with thee!
> (As cited in Bartlett, *Familiar Quotations*, p. 622.)

As I Have Loved You

ELDER ROBERT L. BACKMAN

Fern attended high school in a small town. She was one of those nice but unnoticed girls who don't become much but a face on a yearbook page and a name on the rolls. Her family was poor, and they lived out of town. She was not part of the "in crowd," and the only time her name came up in a conversation of other students was in that mocking, sarcastic way that seems funny when you are young, insecure, and need to ridicule someone else to take the pressure off yourself. Her name became synonymous with anything dumb or out of style. If a thing was unacceptable or ridiculous, the students called it "Ferny."

Young people can be so cruel.

It was an annual tradition in the school to recognize the student who showed the most school spirit and support for the athletic teams. When the assembly came to honor that student, as expected, they called out the name of one of the more popular girls in the school. She bounced up the aisle smiling and waving to all her friends. But then a miracle happened. As she took the stage, she said, "I can't accept this award. Yes, I have loved the teams and cheered for them at every game. But Fern has come to every game, too. I came in a nice, warm car surrounded by my happy friends. She came alone and walked all the way — two-and-a-half miles — sometimes in the rain or snow. She had to sit by herself, but I don't know anyone who cheered with as much spirit as Fern. I would like to nominate her for the most enthusiastic student in the school."

Fern was escorted to the stage to a spontaneous standing ovation from her fellow students.

Youth can be so kind.

Fern is a mature woman today, her hair streaked with gray. Many things have happened to shape her life, but nothing more important than that outburst of acceptance and appreciation from her peers on that memorable day.

And there are mature men and women today who can't remember how many games their teams won or lost that year, but who have never forgotten the warm feeling they had when they stood up and cheered for Fern and welcomed her into their friendship and society.

Attending a stake conference in the Lancaster California Stake, I heard Marianne Mortensen, a lovely Laurel, tell this story as she developed the theme of showing charity toward our peers.

Reaching out to others is not an easy thing to do, particularly when you are young. To take the hand of another at the risk of your own popularity takes a mature, Christlike love. Yet our Savior made no distinction between young and old when he declared, "As I have loved you, . . . love one another." (John 13:34.) How desperately we need that kind of caring in our world today!

Young people are being hit on all sides by open and subtle attacks on their faith, their ideals, their morality, their self-confidence, even their identity. The typical teenager is pictured as being of the *"me"* generation: self-centered, turned inward, unfeeling toward others, seeking immediate self-gratification. Though some young people might fit that description, and many others are struggling and failing in the battle of life, others are winning in spectacular ways. Young men and women are accomplishing things today we used to assume it took a lifetime to do. In science, literature, the arts, social, civic, and spiritual work, we can point with pride to millions of talented teenagers who have set lofty goals and are working to attain them.

The question is, How can we help those who are stumbling to lock arms with those who are striding confidently up the road of life?

"Positive peer pressure," as the social scientists call it, may be the salvation of this generation. If this be true, think how admirably suited our Aaronic Priesthood quorums and our Young Women classes are to offer such meaningful service.

In her talk, Marianne said: "Most of us have a difficult time resisting those who have a genuine love for us. Such people have a way of becoming important to us because we know we are genuinely important to them. The cry of youth today is for genuine concern and for meaningful relationships with our peers. . . . And when I speak of meaningful relationships, I think immediately of the Golden Rule, 'Do unto others as you would have them do unto you.'

"As teenagers, that is a difficult thing to do. Charity for those outside of our circle of friends is difficult to comprehend when we feel so comfortable within the confines of our 'group.' But if we look at the life of our Savior, we see that He didn't leave His 'group,' the Apostles, or those friends about Him. He merely opened His arms to all who would listen. He increased His fold. So . . . we do not have to leave our group to learn to care for the feelings of our peers. We just need to open our arms and increase our friendships."

Marianne Mortensen was right on target.

There is another side to this matter of rendering service to others, not just to our peers, and it applies to those of us who are struggling to find our way.

As a boy I sought happiness as the world measures it. I wanted acceptance, position, fame (particularly as an athlete), and wealth. I had none of these. I was very unhappy. I thought happiness was as elusive as a shadow.

It was not until I was called on a mission that I discovered the real key to happiness. To my surprise, despite the discouragement, the disappointments, and the plain hard work associated with my missionary labors, I was happy. It was then I learned that happiness is really a by-product of service. As I forgot my own desires, my own weaknesses and frailties in my missionary service, I began to understand King Benjamin's profound counsel to his people. "And behold, I tell you these things that ye may learn wisdom; that ye may learn that when ye are in the service of your fellow beings ye are only in the service of your God." (Mosiah 2:17.)

That is why a missionary can return from the toughest experiences of his life and report, "These have been the happiest two years of my life."

A life can never be happy that is focused inward. So if you are miserable now, forget your troubles. March right out your door and find someone who needs you.

You want happiness? Find ways to serve. Your happiness will be commensurate with the service you render.

Just think how much that joy can grow as we expand our love and service to more and more people.

Consider the happiness generated in both the giver and the receiver by these examples of service:

1. Youths of the Meridian Idaho East Stake participated in a community "Paint Your Heart Out" service project. One hundred and sixty-four youth split into five teams, and

each team painted one house of an elderly person during a seven-hour period.

2. Concerned for the youth of his ward, a good bishop in Bountiful, Utah, challenged his young people to taste the sweetness of beautiful service. Reluctantly at first, they put aside their entertainment. One project was making quilts for the mentally retarded at the American Fork Training School. Upon completion of their quilts, the girls delivered them. They arrived at the school in time to help feed supper to the "children." And that was an experience. As they left the school, with mashed potatoes, gravy, and assorted vegetables in their hair and on their outfits, one girl, touched by the sweetness of the "child" she had fed, said, "I'll never forget Billy."

3. In one letter to the editor of a newspaper, I read: "One is continually hearing about the 'Terrible Teenagers' with their obnoxious dress and deplorable actions. How refreshing it was to have a most thrilling experience with, yes, four teenagers.

"One evening I was hosting a special guest from New York City. We were on our beautiful Temple Square, admiring the Seagull Monument. As we turned to go, four teenagers approached us. I immediately felt the [in]security of my gentleman guest, when one of the group stepped forward and said, 'Lady, we would like to present you with this rose to make you happy, and hope that you will have a nice evening.'

"There clutched in his hand was a beautiful, long-stemmed American Beauty red rose, with a spray of fern, artistically wrapped in cellophane.

" 'We bought this rose to give to someone, and when we saw you, we thought you were the one.'

"As they turned to leave, I quickly got their names, expressing my most profound appreciation and admiration for their thoughtfulness and kindness to me, which was so unusual, and how I was quite overwhelmed to think that four teenagers would have the desire for such a gracious act, and that no one would appreciate it more than I would, a little grandmother, as I gave each one a big hug." (Irene E. Staples, *Deseret News*, 22 September 1985.)

4. With the knowledge that her little brother had leukemia, Michelle went to Bear River High School sad and despondent. She struggled through the school day, grateful when the dismissal bell rang. As she collected her books, a friend approached, "Michelle, come into the music room with me." Half-heartedly, Michelle accompanied her. Entering the music room, she was surprised to find the entire a cappella choir. In the straightforward manner of youth, they told Michelle they had been fasting for her little brother and wanted her to join them as they prayed together to end their fast.

Emerson said it well: "Serve, and thou shalt be served. If you love and serve men, you cannot, by any hiding or stratagem, escape the remuneration." ("The Sovereignty of Ethics," in *The Complete Writings of Ralph Waldo Emerson*, New York: Wm. H. Wise & Co., 1929, p. 1004.)

Those we serve, we love. We discover that loving someone else deeply is one of the most joyous feelings we can know, and we begin to understand the bounteous love our Father in Heaven has for us.

D. Brent Collette told a stirring story: "Ronny was not just shy; he was downright backward. As a seventeen-year-old high school senior, Ronny had never really had a close friend or done anything that included other people. He was famous for his shyness. He never said anything to anybody, not even a teacher. One look at him told you a great deal of the story — inferiority complex. He slumped over as if to hide his face and seemed to be always looking as his feet.

119

He always sat in the back of the class and would never participate. . . .

"It was because of Ronny's shyness that I was so astonished when he started coming to my Sunday School class. . . .

"His attendance in my class was the result of the personal efforts of a classmate, Brandon Craig, who had recently befriended Ronny. Boy, if there had ever been a mismatch, this was it. Brandon was 'Mr. Social.' A good head taller than Ronny, he was undisputedly the number-one star of our high school athletics program. Brandon was involved in everything and successful at everything. . . . He was just a neat boy.

"Well, Brandon took to little Ronny like glue. Class was obviously painful for Ronny, but Brandon protected him like the king's guard. I played a low profile — no questions, just a quick smile and once a pat on the back. Time seemed to be helping, but I often wondered if Brandon and company (the rest of the class certainly played it right) would ever be able to break the ice. That's why I was so shocked when Brian, the class president, stood before our Sunday School class one Sunday afternoon and boldly announced that Ronny would offer the opening prayer.

"There was a moment of hesitation; then Ronny slowly came to his feet. Still looking at his shoes, he walked to the front of the room. He folded his arms (his head was already bowed). The class was frozen solid. I thought to myself, 'If he does it, we'll all be translated.'

"Then almost at a whisper I heard, 'Our Father in Heaven, thank you for our Sunday School class.' Then silence — long, loud silence! I could feel poor Ronny suffering. Then came a few sniffles and a muffled sob.

" 'Oh, no,' I thought, 'I should be up front where I can help or something.'

"I hurt for him; we all did. I opened an eye and looked up to make my way to Ronny. But Brandon beat me to it. With an eye still open I watched six-foot-four Brandon put his arm around his friend, bend down and put his chin on Ronny's shoulder, then whisper the words of a short, sweet prayer. Ronny struggled for composure, then repeated the prayer.

"But when the prayer was over, Ronny kept his head bowed and added: 'Thank you for Brandon, amen.' He then turned and looked up at his big buddy and said clear enough for all to hear, 'I love you, Brandon.'

"Brandon, who still had his arm around him, responded, 'I love you too, Ronny. And that was fun.'

"And it was, for all of us." ("Ronny's Buddy," *New Era*, May 1983, p. 18.)

Our Primary children sing that glorious song:

> As I have loved you, Love one another,
> This new commandment: Love one another.
> By this shall men know Ye are my disciples,
> If ye have love One to another.
> (*Hymns*, no. 308.)

And therein lies happiness.

121

To Help a Loved One in Need

ELDER RICHARD G. SCOTT

My message is to those of you who have heavy hearts because a son or daughter, husband or wife, has turned from righteousness to pursue evil. Your life is filled with anguish, pain, and, at times, despair. I will tell you how you can be comforted by the Lord.

First, you must recognize two foundation principles:

1. While there are many things you can do to help a loved one in need, there are some things that must be done by the Lord.

2. Also, no enduring improvement can occur without righteous exercise of agency. Do not attempt to override agency. The Lord Himself would not do that. Forced obedience yields no blessings. (See D&C 58:26-33.)

I will suggest seven ways you can help.

First. Love without limitations. When in a dream Lehi partook of the fruit of the tree of life and was filled with joy, his first thought was to share it with each member of his family, including the disobedient. (See 1 Nephi 8:3-4, 12-13.)

Second. Do not condone the transgressions, but extend every hope and support to the transgressor. To his missionary son Corianton, who had violated the law of chastity, Alma said, "Behold, O my son, how great iniquity ye brought upon the Zoramites; for when they saw your conduct, they would not believe in my words." (Alma 39:11.) Then he clarified in careful detail principles which his son had improperly used to justify his acts. Subsequently, that loving father gave this counsel:

"O, my son, I desire that you should deny the justice of God no more. Do not endeavor to excuse yourself in the least point because of your sins, . . . but do you let the justice of God, and his mercy, and his long-suffering have full sway in your heart; and let it bring you down to the dust in humility. . . .

"And now, my son, go thy way, declare the word with truth and soberness." (Alma 42:30-31.) Corianton repented and became a powerful servant.

Third. Teach truth. Nephi taught his brothers: "Whoso would hearken unto the word of God, and would hold fast unto it, they would never perish; neither could the temptations and the fiery darts of the adversary overpower them unto blindness, to lead them away to destruction." (1 Nephi 15:24.)

Then he gave this example of how to teach: "I did exhort them with all the energies of my soul, and with all the faculty which I possessed, that they would give heed to the word of God and remember to keep his commandments always in all things." (1 Nephi 15:25.)

Fourth. Honestly forgive as often as is required. The Lord declared: "If he . . . repenteth in the sincerity of his heart, him shall ye forgive, and I will forgive him also. . . . And as often as my people repent will I forgive them." (Mosiah 26:29-30.)

Fifth. Pray trustingly. "The . . . fervent prayer of a righteous man availeth much." (James 5:16.)

The Master taught: "Whatsoever ye shall ask the Father

in my name, which is right, believing that ye shall receive, behold it shall be given unto you." (3 Nephi 18:20.) "Pray always, and I will pour out my Spirit upon you, and great shall be your blessing." (D&C 19:38.)

Sixth. Keep perspective. When you have done all that you can reasonably do, rest the burden in the hands of the Lord.

When you take a small pebble and place it directly in front of your eye, it takes on the appearance of a mighty boulder. It is all you can see. It becomes all-consuming — like the problems of a loved one that affect your life every waking moment. When the things you realistically can do to help are done, leave the matter in the hands of the Lord and worry no more. Do not feel guilty because you cannot do more. Do not waste your energy on useless worry. The Lord will take the pebble that fills your vision and cast it down among the challenges you will face in your eternal progress. It will then be seen in perspective. In time, you will feel impressions and know how to give further help. You will find more peace and happiness, will not neglect others that need you, and will be able to give greater help because of that eternal perspective.

Abraham labored that his own father would overcome transgression. Despite his best efforts, his father turned to idolatry. Had Abraham let that proper concern for a father consume his every thought, he could not have received this promise: "In thy seed shall all the kindreds of the earth be blessed." (3 Nephi 20:25.)

Some who have overcome serious sin in their own lives blame themselves because of that prior disobedience when a loved one does not respond as desired. Such promptings come from Satan, not from the Lord. Alma could help his son, Corianton, because Alma spoke from a position of strength, knowing that his own sins had been entirely forgiven through repentance.

This is not a doctrinal discourse; rather, it is a personal witness of what I know to be true. At times my wife, Jeanene, and I have had challenges that seemed more difficult than we could possibly face alone. Once she lost a baby girl and nearly her life. Within six weeks, another beloved son was taken home. We pled for help, and it came.

When other challenges have brought us to our knees, we have had confidence that we would receive comfort and guidance, and they came. The Lord opens doors of opportunity and provides the strength each of us needs at difficult times in our life.

You can receive great comfort as you remember the Resurrection and the price paid and the gift given through the Atonement. Ponder what the scriptures teach of those sacred events. Your personal witness of their reality will be strengthened. They must be more than principles you memorized. They must be woven into the very fiber of your being as a bulwark in time of need.

Nephi taught: "For ye have not come thus far save it were by the word of Christ with unshaken faith in him, relying wholly upon the merits of him who is mighty to save.

"Wherefore, ye must press forward with a steadfastness in Christ, having a perfect brightness of hope, and a love of God and of all men. Wherefore, if ye shall press forward, feasting upon the word of Christ and endure to the end, behold, thus saith the Father: Ye shall have eternal life." (2 Nephi 31:19-20.)

He could well have added, "and shall have peace and happiness now." Happiness comes from understanding and living the teachings of the Lord. It comes from not being critical of yourself when you don't accomplish all you want to do.

One last suggestion. Never give up on a loved one, never! We have a loving Father in Heaven. He asks us to worship Him that we may feel His love. He entreats us to love His Son that we may be comforted and strengthened.

Sometimes, we foolishly recite facts about the Father and the Son, mechanically, and—forgive us—preach to them, preen before them, and display our ignorance and pride. Yet they continue to love us perfectly, each one of us, individually. Yes, they are all-powerful and all-knowing; their works extend eternally, yet their love for each of us is personal, knowing, uncompromising, endless, perfect.

I know they live. I know that Jesus is the Christ, our Savior and Redeemer. I love Him with all my soul. He gave His life that we might overcome errors to live eternally. I don't understand how He did it. In my own imperfect way, I try to imagine the incomprehensible burden He felt as He entered into the closing hours of His ministry on earth, knowing that His life had to be completely sinless, without error. He had to provide the perfect atonement for all mankind, each individual, without exception, or not one soul could ever return to the presence of God. He did it. He did it perfectly. Neither He nor His Father will ever fail us—never in all eternity.

KEEPING LIFE'S
DEMANDS IN BALANCE

ELDER M. RUSSELL BALLARD

I have felt in my own life the power of priesthood blessings and the power of the faith and prayers of Church members. For many years, I have given blessings to others. I have fasted and prayed for their well-being and have exercised my faith for their recovery. During a serious illness of my own, I was the recipient of such faith, prayers, and blessings. I am grateful for the prayers that were offered in my behalf.

One of my colleagues said to me that some good would come from the illness. He suggested that it is good, on occasion, for everyone to face adversity, especially if it causes introspection that enables us to openly and honestly assess our lives. That is what I did.

The night before I was to have surgery, my doctors talked about the possibility of cancer. When I was left alone, my mind filled with thoughts of my family and of my ministry. I found comfort in the ordinances of the gospel that bind me to my family if we are faithful. I realized that I needed to rearrange some of my priorities to accomplish the things that matter most to me.

Sometimes we need a personal crisis to reinforce in our minds what we really value and cherish. The scriptures are filled with examples of people facing crises before learning

127

how to better serve God and others. Perhaps if you, too, search your heart and courageously assess the priorities in your life, you may discover, as I did, that you need a better balance among your priorities.

All of us must come to an honest, open self-examination, an awareness within as to who and what we want to be.

Coping with the complex and diverse challenges of everyday life, which is not an easy task, can upset the balance and harmony we seek. Many good people who care a great deal are trying very hard to maintain balance, but they sometimes feel overwhelmed and defeated.

A mother of four small children said: "There is no balance at all in my life. I am completely consumed in trying to raise my children. I hardly have time to think of anything else."

A young father, who felt the pressure of being the family provider, said: "My new business requires all of my time. I realize that I am neglecting my family and church duties, but if I can just get through one more year I will make enough money, and then things will settle down."

A high school student said: "We hear so many contrasting views that it is hard to always know what is right and what is wrong."

How often have we heard this one? "No one knows better than I do how important exercise is, but I just have no time in my day for exercising."

A single parent said: "I find it next to impossible to accomplish all that I need to do to manage my home and lead my family. In fact, sometimes I think the world expects too much of me. Regardless of how hard I work, I never will live up to everyone's expectations."

Another mother of four remarked: "My struggle is between self-esteem, confidence, and feelings of self-worth versus guilt, depression, and discouragement for not doing everything I am told we must do to attain the celestial kingdom."

We all face these kinds of struggles from time to time. They are common human experiences. Many people have heavy demands upon them stemming from parental, family, employment, church, and civic responsibilities. Keeping everything in balance can be a real problem.

A periodic review of the covenants we have made with the Lord will help us with our priorities and with balance in our lives. This review will help us see where we need to repent and change our lives to ensure that we are worthy of the promises that accompany our covenants and sacred ordinances. Working out our own salvation requires good planning and a deliberate, valiant effort.

I have a few suggestions that I hope will be valuable to those concerned with balancing life's demands. These suggestions are very basic; their concepts can easily be overlooked if you are not careful. You will need a strong commitment and personal discipline to incorporate them into your life.

First, think about your life and set your priorities. Find some quiet time regularly to think deeply about where you are going and what you will need to do to get there. Jesus, our exemplar, often "withdrew himself into the wilderness, and prayed." (Luke 5:16.) We need to do the same thing occasionally to rejuvenate ourselves spiritually as the Savior did. Write down the tasks you would like to accomplish each day. Keep foremost in mind the sacred covenants you have made with the Lord as you write down your daily schedule.

Second, set short-term goals that you can reach. Set goals that are well balanced—not too many or too few, and not too high or too low. Write down your attainable goals and work on them according to their importance. Pray for divine guidance in setting goals.

You recall that Alma said he would like to be an angel so he could "speak with the trump of God, . . . to shake the earth, and cry repentance unto every people!" (Alma 29:1.) He then said, "But behold, I am a man, and do sin in my wish; for I ought to be content with the things which the Lord hath allotted unto me. . . .

"Why should I desire more than to perform the work to which I have been called?" (Alma 29:3, 6.)

Third, everyone faces financial challenges in life. Through wise budgeting, control your real needs and measure them carefully against your many wants in life. Far too many individuals and families have incurred too much debt. Be careful of the many attractive offers to borrow money. It is much easier to borrow money than it is to pay it back. There are no shortcuts to financial security. There are no get-rich-quick schemes that work. Perhaps none need the principle of balance in their lives more than those who are driven toward accumulating "things" in this world.

Do not trust your money to others without a thorough evaluation of any proposed investment. Our people have lost far too much money by trusting their assets to others. In my judgment, we never will have balance in our lives unless our finances are securely under control.

The prophet Jacob said to his people: "Wherefore, do not spend money for that which is of no worth, nor your labor for that which cannot satisfy. Hearken diligently unto me, and remember the words which I have spoken; and come unto the Holy One of Israel, and feast upon that which perisheth not, neither can be corrupted, and let your soul delight in fatness." (2 Nephi 9:51.)

Remember to always pay a full tithing.

Fourth, stay close to your spouse, children, relatives,

and friends. They will help you keep a balance in your life. In one study conducted by the Church, adults in the United States were asked to identify a time when they were very happy and to describe the experience. They were also asked to describe a time when they were very unhappy. For most people, one thing that had made them the most happy or the most sad was their personal relationships with others. Much less important were their personal health, employment, money, and other material things. Build relationships with your family and friends through open and honest communication.

A good marriage and good family relationships can be maintained through gentle, loving, thoughtful communication. Remember that often a glance, a wink, a nod, or a touch will say more than words. A sense of humor and good listening are also vital parts of good communication.

Fifth, study the scriptures. They offer one of the best sources we have to keep in touch with the Spirit of the Lord. One of the ways I have gained my sure knowledge that Jesus is the Christ is through my study of the scriptures. President Ezra Taft Benson has called upon members of the Church to make the study of the Book of Mormon a daily habit and a lifetime pursuit. The Apostle Paul's advice to Timothy is good counsel for each of us. He wrote: "From a child thou hast known the holy scriptures, which are able to make thee wise unto salvation through faith which is Christ Jesus.

"All scripture is given by inspiration of God, and is profitable for doctrine, for reproof, for correction, for instruction in righteousness." (2 Timothy 3:15-16.)

Sixth, many people, including me, have difficulty finding the time for sufficient rest, exercise, and relaxation. We must schedule time on our daily calendars for these activities if we are to enjoy a healthy and balanced life. Good physical appearance enhances our dignity and self-respect.

Seventh, the prophets have taught repeatedly that families should teach one another the gospel, preferably in a weekly family home evening. This family practice, if we are not very careful, can slowly drift away from us. We must not lose this special opportunity to "teach one another the doctrine of the kingdom" (D&C 88:77), which will lead families to eternal life.

Satan is always working to destroy our testimonies, but he will not have the power to tempt or disturb us beyond our strength to resist when we are studying the gospel and living its commandments.

My last suggestion is to pray often as individuals and as families. Parents need to exercise the discipline required to lead out and motivate children to join together for regular family prayers. Our youth can know the right decisions to make each day through constant, sincere prayer.

The prophet Alma summarized the importance of prayer in these words: "But that ye would humble yourselves before the Lord, and call on his holy name, and watch and pray continually, that ye may not be tempted above that which ye can bear, and thus be led by the Holy Spirit, becoming humble, meek, submissive, patient, full of love and all long-suffering." (Alma 13:28.) When I am in tune spiritually, I find that I can balance everything in my life much more easily.

Other suggestions could be added to these. However, I believe that when we focus on a few basic objectives, we are more likely to be able to manage the many demands that life makes on us. Remember, too much of anything in life can throw us off balance. At the same time, too little of the important things can do the same thing. King Benjamin counseled "that all these things are done in wisdom and order." (Mosiah 4:27.)

Often the lack of clear direction and goals can waste away our time and energy and contribute to imbalance in our lives. A life that gets out of balance is much like a car tire that is out of balance. It will make the operation of the car rough and unsafe. Tires in perfect balance can give a smooth and comfortable ride. So it is with life. The ride through mortality can be smoother for us when we strive to stay in balance. Our main goal should be to seek "immortality and eternal life." (Moses 1:39.) With this as our goal, why not eliminate from our lives the things that clamor for and consume our thoughts, feelings, and energies without contributing to our reaching that goal?

Just a word to Church leaders: Be very careful that what you ask from members will help them attain eternal life. For Church members to be able to balance their lives, Church leaders must be sure they do not require so much from members that they have no time to accomplish their personal and family goals.

Not long ago, one of my children said, "Dad, sometimes I wonder if I will ever make it." The answer I gave to her is the same as I would give to you if you have had similar feelings. Just do the very best you can each day. Do the basic things and, before you realize it, your life will be full of spiritual understanding that will confirm to you that your Heavenly Father loves you. When a person knows this, then life will be full of purpose and meaning, making balance easier to maintain.

THE ROYAL ROAD TO HAPPINESS

ELDER J. RICHARD CLARKE

I recall a story about Chief Justice Oliver Wendell Holmes. He was riding a train. When the conductor came by to pick up his ticket, he could not find it. Recognizing the Chief Justice, the conductor said, "I'm sure, Mr. Holmes, that you'll be able to find your ticket when you return home. I'm certain that the Pennsylvania Railroad can get by without that ticket until you find it. Why don't you just mail it to us?"

"Young man, you don't understand at all," he said. "The problem is not where is my ticket; it's where am I going?"

Each of us has a challenge to identify where we are going. In the Book of Abraham when the gods were preparing the plan for the spirit children to come forward and continue their education, they said: "We will prove them herewith, to see if they will do all things whatsoever the Lord their God shall command them;

"And they who keep their first estate shall be added upon; . . . and they who keep their second estate shall have glory added upon their heads for ever and ever." (Abraham 3:25-26.)

We are here on earth because we were faithful in our first estate. We learned to keep the laws that magnified us for future opportunity. We were indeed added upon and have entered our second estate with a successful record of performance. Just like an advancement from high school to the university, the pace of the second estate is quicker than that of the first. We are learning to achieve the promised glories, and we must lengthen our strides. Now that we have the desires of the flesh to subdue, we must once again master the laws that bring us joy in this life and the glories of eternity. Once again, we must be proven in all things.

The Prophet Joseph Smith said that "happiness is the object and design of our existence." (*History of the Church,* 5:134.) Much has been said about the pursuit of happiness, but not quite so much about the happiness of pursuit. We must vigorously pursue that which enlarges our vision. We must, in fact, get on the offensive. Phillips Brooks once wrote, "Bad will be the day for every man when he becomes absolutely contented with the life that he is living, with the thoughts that he is thinking, with the deeds that he is doing; when there is not forever beating at the door of his soul some great desire to do something larger." To the Philippians Paul said: "This one thing I do, forgetting those things which are behind, and reaching forth unto those things which are before,

"I press toward the mark." (Philippians 3:13-14.)

If happiness is the object and design of our existence, it seems to me that we must set some criteria for achieving it. One of the great souls of this generation was a philosopher by the name of William George Jordan, whose son, David Starr Jordan, was at one time president of Stanford University. He wrote an impressive essay, titled "The Royal Road to Happiness," in which he said:

> There is a royal road to happiness; it lies in Consecration, Concentration, Conscience, and Conquest. Consecration is dedicating the individual life to the service of others, to some

135

noble mission, to realize some unselfish ideal. Concentration makes the individual life simpler and deeper. It cuts away the shams and the pretenses of modern living and limits life to its truest essentials. Worry, fear, useless regret—all the great wastes that sap mental, moral or physical energy—must be sacrificed, or the individual needlessly destroys half the possibilities of living. Conscience, as the mentor, the guide and compass of every act, leads ever to Happiness. When the individual can stay alone with his conscience and get its approval, without using force or specious logic, then he begins to know what real Happiness is. Conquest is the overcoming of an evil habit, the rising superior to opposition and attack, the spiritual exaltation that comes from resisting the invasion of the grovelling material side of life. (William George Jordan, *The Majesty of Calmness*, Old Tappan, N.J.: F. H. Revell, n.d., pp. 51-53.)

I would like to touch briefly on each of these four points.

CONSECRATION

President Spencer W. Kimball indicated that perhaps the number-one problem we face is that of selfishness. The happiest people I know are those who have developed an acute sensitivity to the feelings and needs of other people. President Kimball was a personification of those great impulses.

Dr. Karl Menninger, the psychologist, was once asked by a lady, "If you knew for a certainty that you were going to have a nervous breakdown, what would you do?"

He said, "I would close my house; I would move over onto the other side of the tracks; I would knock on doors until I had an opportunity to meet somebody who had more problems than I did; and then I'd spend my time helping them solve those problems."

We read about bread being cast upon the water. There is a great multiplier effect in people's willingness to give of themselves that others might be blessed. Consider the situation of one mother in the nineteenth-century frontier of Kentucky. Life was rough for Sally Bush Johnston. She was left a widow with three children. She was getting older before she wanted to, and certainly hers was a much more difficult existence than she had ever imagined. Then she saw a chance for an easier life when an old friend of hers, a suitor she had known before she married and who was now a widower, came courting. He was dressed in a fine suit and a new pair of boots. He spoke of prosperity, of farming. He spoke of servants and of a way of life that seemed to be an improvement over that which she was experiencing. So she went with him.

When she got there, she found the "prosperous" farm to be a ramshackle, run-down farm covered with wild black-berry bushes and sumac. The house was a floorless hut—a log cabin, in fact, without windows. The only evidence of servants was two small children, a boy and a girl.

Her first thought was an obvious one: "I can't stay. I've got to return." She knew she had been duped. But as she turned to leave, she looked at the children, especially the younger—a boy whose thin face and melancholy gaze made upon her soul an impression as deep as it was instantaneous. At that moment a great spirit subdued her disappointment. She slipped off her sweater and began to straighten and clean the house. In determined words that she felt deeply within her, she said quietly, "I'll stay for the sake of this boy."

A neighbor was to write sometime later, "Oh, Sally Bush, what a treasure trembled in the balance that day." But Sally Bush could not have known that her stepson, this young boy whose melancholy eyes had penetrated her heart, was to become the President of the United States, states remaining "united" through a tragic civil war that would claim his life among the numbered dead. Sally Bush Lincoln, discouraged and tired and disappointed, looked into the eyes of a ten-year-old boy and said, "I'll stay for the sake of this boy."

In another place and another time, a wealthy family in England was spending the weekend with another wealthy family. Their son fell into a swimming pool and was in the process of drowning when the screams of the children attracted the attention of a gardener who plunged into the pool and saved the boy.

The boy's name was Winston Churchill. His parents, deeply grateful, attempted to reward the gardener. At first the man hesitated, but as they insisted he said, "I have a son whose dream is to be a doctor, and I don't know how we can provide that opportunity for him."

Mr. Churchill replied, "We will see him through and pay for his education."

Later on, when Winston Churchill became prime minister of Great Britain, he contracted a severe case of pneumonia. Word was sent out that he needed the finest physician to attend him. Sir Alexander Fleming, the developer of penicillin, was called and selected to care for the prime minister. He was also the son of the gardener. Churchill was to later say: "Rarely has one man owed his life twice to the same person." (*Bits and Pieces*, August 1979.)

Many people, I suppose, fantasize that if they were blessed with great wealth they would generously share with those who are in need. But that is unlikely unless they already give of themselves to those with whom they serve while living from day to day.

CONCENTRATION

The ability to concentrate is a mark of genius. Certainly we ought to focus our lives on the essentials. We ought to set high goals and meet high standards of performance. We ought to live with anticipation.

One of the sweetest people I know is Margaret Wells, a widow for over forty-five years, the wife of John Wells who was formerly second counselor in the Presiding Bishopric. She once told me, "I never go to bed at night until I can think of at least one good reason for waking up in the morning, at least one important job that I have to do. Even if it's only one thing, I wake up with anticipation. I look forward to getting up. If I waited until morning to plan my work, I'm afraid I'd just lie there and not put forth much effort."

I would suggest that we learn to wait to worry. Just about every time you get bad news, chances are that it has either already happened and you cannot do anything about it, or it was not worth worrying about in the first place. Psychologists have estimated that just 14 percent of all the bad news we initially hear is even worth the worry at all. We would do well to wait to worry.

I am impressed with how important attitude is in our lives. No matter how old we are or how educated we are, we are still mightily affected, both positively and negatively, by our attitude. I remember the story of a man who worked with refrigerator cars. One day he got himself locked inside of a car. Understanding what usually happens in such circumstances, he began to prepare himself to freeze to death. As he felt his body becoming numb, he recorded the story of his approaching death on the walls of the refrigerator car. He scribbled: "I'm becoming colder. . . . Still colder now. . . . Nothing to do but wait. . . . I am slowly freezing to death. . . . Half asleep now, I can hardly write. . . . [And finally] These may be my last words."

And they were. He died. Yet those who opened the car found that at no time had it been colder than 56 degrees. The refrigeration apparatus had malfunctioned. This man was the victim of his own illusion. All his conclusions were wrong. He knew about refrigeration; he knew what happened. He just failed to understand that, in this particular case, the refrigeration apparatus was not working. The mind has great power over and produces magical effects on the body.

CONSCIENCE

Conscience is our contact with the Spirit. Spiritual power is the greatest form of energy that I know. Spiritual power alone can sustain us in a time of crisis. Ethics are not enough. Spiritual power comes from God and is administered and controlled upon principles of righteousness. Our goal, as Peter advises us, is to be "partakers of the divine nature of Christ." One way to do so is by "escaping the corruption that is in the world through lust." (2 Peter 1:4.)

Jesus warned about those who might destroy our bodies but then explained that the real problem is he who can destroy both body and spirit. The adversary is ever with us. He tries to tempt us, to destroy our lives, to convince us of incorrect and unsound and untrue principles that so often take us off course.

Consider the encounter Moses had with the adversary. "Satan came tempting him, saying: Moses, son of man, worship me.

"And it came to pass that Moses looked upon Satan and said: Who art thou? For behold, I am a son of God, in the similitude of his Only Begotten; and where is thy glory, that I should worship thee? . . .

"Get thee hence, Satan; deceive me not; for God said unto me: Thou art after the similitude of my Only Begotten." (Moses 1:12-13, 16.)

We would do well, when tempted, to simply run those words through our minds: "Satan, why should I worship you? Where is your glory? I am a son (or daughter) of God created in the image and likeness of Him who saved the world." I am impressed by D&C 20:22, which says of the Savior, "He suffered temptations but gave no heed unto them."

President Heber J. Grant said: "We have no right to go near temptation, or in fact to do or say a thing that we cannot honestly ask the blessings of the Lord upon, neither to visit any place where we would be ashamed to take our sister or sweetheart. The good spirit will not go with us on the devil's ground, and if we are standing alone upon the ground belonging to the adversary of men's souls, he may have the power to trip us up and destroy us. . . . Virtue is more valuable than life. Never allow yourself to go out of curiosity to see any of the undercrust in this world. We can't handle dirty things and keep our hands clean." (Bruce B. Clark, *Richard Evans' Quote Book,* Salt Lake City: Publishers Press, 1971, p. 201.)

The mother of John and Charles Wesley counseled them by saying: "Would you judge the lawfulness or unlawfulness of pleasure? Take this rule: . . . Whatever weakens your reason, impairs the tenderness of your spirit, obscures your sense of God, takes off your relish for spiritual things, whatever increases the authority of the body over the mind, that thing is sin to you, however innocent it may seem in itself."

A number of years ago I attended a management training seminar in New York. During a coffee break everyone in the room left except the instructor and myself. I inquired, "Don't you drink coffee?"

"No," he said.

"Well, that's interesting," I said. "You'd better be careful, or they'll be accusing you of being a Mormon."

"No, I'm a Baptist. But years ago I made a decision about my life and it was that I would do nothing which would take away from me my freedom. As of that time, I quit smoking, drinking, and taking any kind of intoxicants or anything that's addictive."

What a marvelous reason to abstain from anything that might be of harm to us! It takes away our freedom.

Zig Ziglar wrote: "To build a healthy self-image, there are some things you must avoid. Pornography is the primary one. Literally everything that goes into your mind has an effect and is permanently recorded. It either builds and prepares you for the future or it tears down and reduces your accomplishment possibilities for the future. Psychologists say that three viewings of Deep Throat, The Last Tango in Paris, The Exorcist, or any of the 'X-rated' films or television programs have the same psychological, emotional, destructive impact on your minds as one physical experience. The people who have seen these 'shows' are in agreement; they were sexually stimulated and viewed themselves with less respect. The reason is simple. These films or programs present mankind at its worst and when you see your fellow man degraded, you, in effect, see yourself degraded. It is impossible to view mankind at its worst and not feel that your own value has diminished and you can neither be nor do any better than you think you can or are. Ironically most X-rated films are advertised as 'adult' entertainment for 'mature' audiences. Most psychologists agree that they are juvenile entertainment for immature and insecure audiences." (See You at the Top, Pelican, 1984.)

What is the harmful effect of sin upon the soul? Sin places the sinner in bondage. Sin enslaves the sinner by making him love sinful things.

Karl Menninger says: "The wrongness of the sinful act lies not merely in its nonconformity, its departure from the accepted, appropriate way of behavior, but in an implicitly aggressive quality—a ruthlessness, a hurting, a breaking away from God and from the rest of humanity, a partial alienation, or act of rebellion.

"Standing on one's head is nonconforming, and it is neither aesthetic nor congenial behavior nor expressive of a moral ideal, but it is not likely to be considered sinful. Sin has a willful, defiant, or disloyal quality; someone is defied or offended or hurt. The willful disregard or sacrifice of the welfare of others for the welfare or satisfaction of the self is an essential quality of the concept of sin. . . . And sin is thus, at heart, a refusal of the love of others." (Karl Menninger, *Whatever Became of Sin?* New York: Hawthorn Books, 1973, p. 19.)

CONQUEST

Habits are an enemy to progress. Confucius said that the nature of men is always the same; it is their habits that separate them. The power to change, the power to banish the desire for evil practice or the fierceness from our hearts, comes through the Lord Jesus Christ. We must experience a godly sorrow (as we are told in Alma 36) if we are to be forgiven of the sins we want blotted from our memory and from our heart. We must come to terms with the Lord's anointed, our bishops, and through proper confession obtain a full and lasting forgiveness.

I am interested in a psychologist's point of view of the need for confession. "Confession must include a recognition of the aggression of the sins committed. 'So long as a person lives under the shadow of real, unacknowledged, and unexpiated guilt, . . . he . . . will continue to hate himself and to suffer the inevitable consequences of self-hatred. But the moment he . . . begins to accept his guilt and his sinfulness, the possibility of radical reformation opens up; and . . . a new freedom of self-respect and peace.' " (O. Hobart Mowrer, quoted by Menninger, *Whatever Became of Sin?*, p. 195.)

So all habits, then, are a challenge. Elder Delbert L. Stapley once said that we are not born into this life with fixed habits any more than we are born with noble character, and that when anybody boasts about his bad habits one can be sure that they are the best he has. The only way we can pay the price is to be motivated to have the blessing that accompanies the change. Remember, if bulls had no horns, anybody could be a matador.

We are so fortunate as members of The Church of Jesus Christ of Latter-day Saints to understand the great power of redemption. Through the Lord Jesus Christ we can be and are redeemed. We are able to enjoy peace of mind and the beauties of the hope and the fulfillment of lives in harmony with sound and basic principles and values. Is it worth it?

Recently I was reading in the third chapter of Malachi the scripture to which we often refer as an explanation of the Lord's law of tithing.

"Ye have said, It is vain to serve God: and what profit is it that we have kept his ordinance, and that we have walked mournfully before the Lord of hosts?

"And now we call the proud happy: yea, they that work wickedness are set up; yea, they that tempt God are even delivered. [In other words, "How come everybody else who doesn't keep these commandments gets along so well?"]

[And then the Lord says:] "Then they that feared the Lord spake often one to another: and the Lord hearkened, and heard it, and a book of remembrance was written before him for them that feared the Lord, and that thought upon his name.

"And they shall be mine, saith the Lord of hosts, in that day when I make up my jewels; and I will spare them, as a man spareth his own son that serveth him.

"Then shall ye return, and discern between the righteous

144

and the wicked, between him that serveth God and him that serveth him not." (Malachi 3:14-18.)

If we would in fact be happy and enjoy the blessings of eternal life, we must remember these words: "And moreover, I would desire that ye should consider on the blessed and happy state of those that keep the commandments of God. For behold, they are blessed in all things, both temporal and spiritual; and if they hold out faithful to the end they are received into heaven, that thereby they may dwell with God in a state of never-ending happiness. O remember, remember that these things are true; for the Lord hath spoken it." (Mosiah 2:41.)

HAPPINESS

ELDER JACK H. GOASLIND

One summer day I saw an interesting picture as I followed a car on the freeway. It was a large station wagon that had obviously endured many road skirmishes. The top rack was loaded with luggage; the seats were loaded with people. Four bare feet hung out the rear window, and elbows and arms hung out the side windows. In the front seat, the mother was wrestling with a feisty child while simultaneously trying to calm an upset infant. The father was desperately trying to negotiate the heavy traffic. It was obviously vacation time for this family. As I surveyed the situation with some degree of empathy, I noticed a bumper sticker which read, "Are we having fun yet?"

I laugh about this scene whenever I recall it. I believe it is amusing because it exhibits a wry insight into human nature. It reveals a very real aspect of the human condition: the largely unfulfilled pursuit of happiness. The implications of the question "Are we having fun yet?" are profound. How many people in this world pursue happiness but find that it eludes them? They contrive pleasures, invent amusements, and invest heavily in recreation. They go abroad in search of this rare gift but fail to see that evidence of it is all around them; the source is within them.

146

As I have occasion to be with wonderful people throughout the world, I am often moved by the many individuals I meet who are looking for happiness, but not quite finding it. They yearn and strive and endure, but seem to be asking, "Am I happy yet?" I desire to assure you that happiness is real. It can be experienced here, and we can know a fulness of joy in the hereafter. May I share with you some insights about the kind of happiness promised by the gospel of Jesus Christ.

Lehi's words to his son Jacob include a profound truth: "All things have been done in the wisdom of him who knoweth all things. Adam fell that man might be; and men are, that they might have joy." (2 Nephi 2:24-25.)

Our wise and loving Father in Heaven is concerned for the welfare of His children. He desires to see us happy. The very purpose of our lives can be defined in terms of happiness. The Prophet Joseph Smith said, "Happiness is the object and design of our existence; and will be the end thereof, if we pursue the path that leads to it." (*History of the Church*, 5:134.)

Our yearnings for happiness were implanted in our hearts by Deity. They represent a kind of homesickness, for we have a residual memory of our premortal existence. They are also a foretaste of the fulness of joy that is promised to the faithful. We can expect with perfect faith that our Father will fulfill our innermost longings for joy. In fact, the plan he has given to guide us is called "the plan of happiness." (Alma 42:16.) In the meridian of time, it was heralded by angelic messengers as "good tidings of great joy, which shall be to all people." (Luke 2:10.)

The Book of Mormon makes it clear that happiness is our destiny. It speaks of dwelling "with God in a state of never-ending happiness." (Mosiah 2:41.) It is also made clear that "all things shall be restored to their proper order, every thing to its natural frame, . . . raised to endless happiness to inherit the kingdom of God, or to endless misery to inherit the kingdom of the devil." (Alma 41:4.) We also learn that we are "raised to happiness according to [our] desires of happiness." (Alma 41:5.)

Words such as *reap, restored,* and *desire* imply that happiness is a consequence, not a reward. We are *restored* to a state of happiness when we have chosen to live according to the plan of happiness. Our joy in God's kingdom will be a natural extension of the happiness we cultivate in this life.

Our happiness is diminished by at least two things: sin and adversity. Of the two, sin is the most tragic. Sin is the most persistent cause of human suffering and of the two brings the deepest remorse. Sin and the temptation to do evil are part of our mortal test. We are being tried to see if we will choose good or evil. It is a hard test, and only those who have resisted temptation can know and gain the strength thereof. Sin is sin because it destroys instead of saves; it tears down instead of builds; it causes despair instead of hope.

The Book of Mormon speaks of men that are in a "carnal state . . . and in the bonds of iniquity; they are without God in the world, and they have gone contrary to the nature of God; therefore, they are in a state contrary to the nature of happiness." (Alma 41:11.) It also records Samuel the Lamanite's warning to the Nephites: "Ye have sought all the days of your lives for that which ye could not obtain; and ye have sought for happiness in doing iniquity, which thing is contrary to the nature of that righteousness which is in our great and Eternal Head." (Helaman 13:38.)

The doctrine is concisely summarized by Alma: "Behold, I say unto you, *wickedness never was happiness.*" (Alma 41:10; italics added.) If we are not pure, we would be miserable

148

in the presence of God and Christ, who are by their very nature happy and joyful and cannot look upon sin with any allowance.

The suffering that results from sin is most tragic because through our own choices we can choose to avoid it. We have that power. We also have the capacity to repent of our sins and to experience the sweet joy of forgiveness. If we are unhappy, let us examine ourselves to see where we need to repent. If we have questions about what we need to do, or not do, we need only listen to our conscience and follow the promptings of the Spirit.

I am acquainted with a man who rebelled from the Church when he was a youth. He made some mistakes during this time and developed some habits. Eventually, however, he came to himself; he served a mission and returned home to hold many responsible positions in the Church. But he was never quite happy. He could have said as did Nephi:

"I am encompassed about, because of the temptations and the sins which do so easily beset me. And when I desire to rejoice, my heart groaneth because of my sins." (2 Nephi 4:18-19.)

Finally, in a night of spiritual turmoil, the man confessed to himself that he had never fully forsaken his sins. Although he had not committed sins worthy of Church court action, he still harbored attitudes and thoughts that robbed him of spirituality, and he went through cycles of guilt and despair that dampened his happiness. He made up his mind to change, and he kept his resolve. He broke the chain of sin and despair and, for the first time in memory, began to experience a real, true happiness. If someone had asked him, "Are we having fun, experiencing happiness, yet?" he could have answered, "Yes, more happiness, or joy, than I could have imagined."

Striving for happiness is a long, hard journey with many challenges. It requires eternal vigilance to win the victory. You cannot succeed with sporadic little flashes of effort. Constant and valiant living is necessary. That is why patience and faith are so often associated in the scriptures. You must "withstand every temptation of the devil, with [your] faith on the Lord Jesus Christ." (Alma 37:33.) But remember, faith is not a magical formula. It requires that you make a deliberate decision to do good and then carry out your decision. Do it. Simply do it, and do it long enough that you experience success, no matter how hard it may seem. Your victory over self brings communion with God and results in happiness — lasting and eternal happiness.

The other thing that may diminish our happiness is adversity. Adversity is also part of our mortal probation, experienced by everyone. It is different, however, from sin. While we can choose to avoid sin, we usually cannot choose whether we experience adversity. I am convinced if we are to have happiness in our hearts, we must learn how to preserve it, in our hearts, in the midst of trouble and trial. We can control our attitude toward adversity. Some people are defeated and embittered by it, while others triumph over it and cultivate godlike attributes in the midst of it.

I recall a true story from our pioneer heritage that illustrates how we can choose our response to adversity. Over one hundred years ago a Swedish family who had joined the Church faced a long ocean voyage to America, a train trip from New York to Omaha, and then a trek by wagon train to Salt Lake City. During their train trip they rode in stock cars used to haul hogs. The cars were filthy and filled with hog lice. On their wagon trip across the plains, a healthy baby was born, but their three-year-old contracted cholera. During the night, the father went to a neighboring wagon to borrow a candle, but was told they couldn't spare one. This angered him, and he fumed as he sat in the dark with his son's limp, feverish body in his arms. The boy died that night.

The next morning the wagon master said they would hold a short funeral and bury the boy in a shallow grave. They were in Indian country and didn't have time to do more. The father insisted on staying behind and digging a grave deep enough so the animals would not disturb the body. They experienced other hardships before they reached Salt Lake City.

Both the mother and the father experienced the same trials, but the father became withdrawn, cantankerous, and bitter. He stopped going to church, found fault with Church leaders. He became caught up in his own miseries, and the light of Christ grew dimmer and dimmer in his life.

On the other hand, the mother's faith increased. Each new problem seemed to make her stronger. She became an angel of mercy—filled with empathy, compassion, and charity. She was a light to those around her. Her family gravitated toward her and looked to her as their leader. She was happy; he was miserable. (See *Ensign,* February 1981, pp. 54-55.)

I would offer one key to maintaining your happiness in spite of adversity. Christ said, "For whosoever will save his life shall lose it: but whosoever will lose his life for my sake, the same shall save it." (Luke 9:24.) If you would find happiness and joy, lose your life in some noble cause. A worthy purpose must be at the center of every worthy life. President Stephen L Richards noted that life is a mission, not a career. (See *Where Is Wisdom,* Salt Lake City: Deseret Book Co., 1955, p. 74.) As Church members, our mission should be the greatest, noblest mission in the universe— the salvation of souls.

President David O. McKay was fond of quoting the poet

Robert Browning, who said, "There is an answer to the passionate longings of the heart for fullness, and I knew it, and the answer is this: Live in all things outside yourself by love, and you will have joy. That is the life of God; it ought to be our life. In him it is accomplished and perfect; but in all created things it is a lesson learned slowly and through difficulty." (Quoted in *Stepping Stones to an Abundant Life,* comp. Llewelyn R. McKay, Salt Lake City: Deseret Book Co., 1971, p. 119.)

Service helps us forget our own travails; it enlarges our souls and gives us greater capacity to endure our own trials.

Now, I have written of our Father's plan of happiness by which He guides us into eternal joy. I have discussed overcoming sin through repentance and self-mastery, and I have mentioned taking the edge off of adversity through selfless service. Self-mastery and service are keys to our Father's plan. Christ told His disciples:

"If ye keep my commandments, ye shall abide in my love. . . . These things I have spoken unto you, that my joy might remain in you, and that your joy might be full." (John 15:10-11.)

The commandments are guides to happiness. I implore you to follow them.

"Are we having fun yet, experiencing true happiness?" I certainly am. I find great joy in life in obeying and serving. It is my prayer that you may also discover the elusive treasure of true happiness through the means that were ordained by our Father.

Patience, a Key to Happiness

ELDER JOSEPH B. WIRTHLIN

One of the greatest sentences to fall upon human ears comes from the Book of Mormon: "Adam fell that men might be; and men are, that they might have joy." (2 Nephi 2:25.) That sentence captures the major possibilities of life. Let me add, we will have genuine joy and happiness only as we learn patience.

Dictionaries define *patience* in such terms as bearing pain or sorrow calmly or without complaint; not being hasty or impetuous; being steadfast despite opposition, difficulty, or adversity.

In a passage from the Book of Mormon, Alma helps us understand patience. After telling about planting a seed that can grow to become a tree, he adds these insightful words: "And behold, as the tree beginneth to grow, . . . if ye nourish it with much care it will get root, and grow up, and bring forth fruit. . . .

"And because of your diligence and your faith and your patience . . . ye shall pluck the fruit thereof, which is most precious, which is sweet above all that is sweet, . . . and ye shall feast upon this fruit even until ye are filled, that ye hunger not, neither shall ye thirst. . . .

"Ye shall reap the rewards of your faith, and your diligence, and your patience." (Alma 32:37, 42-43.)

I don't know whether we Church members fully appreciate the Book of Mormon, one of our sacred scriptures, as we really should. One of the clearest explanations of why we need patience to endure the trials of life is set forth in these striking words: "For it must needs be, that there is an opposition in all things. If not so, . . . righteousness could not be brought to pass, neither wickedness, neither holiness nor misery, neither good nor bad. Wherefore, all things must needs be a compound in one. . . .

"And if ye shall say there is no law, ye shall also say there is no sin, ye shall also say there is no righteousness. And if there be no righteousness there be no happiness. And if there be no righteousness nor happiness there be no punishment nor misery. And if these things are not there is no God. And if there is no God we are not, neither the earth; for there could have been no creation of things, neither to act nor to be acted upon; wherefore, all things must have vanished away." (2 Nephi 2:11, 13.)

The Apostle Paul gave the purpose of patience in his epistle to the Saints in Rome: "We glory in tribulations . . . knowing that tribulation worketh patience;

"And patience, experience; and experience, hope." (Romans 5:3-4.)

In 1947 President J. Reuben Clark, Jr., a member of the First Presidency, gave an address titled "Slipping from Our Old Moorings." He described how we have slipped away from living the Ten Commandments. (See *Church News*, 8 March 1947, pp. 1, 8-9.)

If we had slipped away then, where are we now? In 1947, television and computers were in their infancies. We had no satellite broadcasts or videotapes and no computer fraud. Certainly our moral standards of decency and propriety have slipped from where they were in 1947. The obscenity, nudity, and other forms of pornography that would have made us blush and turn away in shame in 1947 are now thrust at us openly in printed and audiovisual material. They are even paraded through our homes unless we are careful to keep them out. As a people, we are slipping further from our old moorings today because we are not following our prophets.

A certain amount of impatience may be useful to stimulate and motivate us to action. However, I believe that a lack of patience is a major cause of the difficulties and unhappiness in the world today. Too often, we are impatient with ourselves, with our family members and friends, and even with the Lord. We seem to demand what we want right now, regardless of whether we have earned it, whether it would be good for us, or whether it is right. Some seek immediate gratification or numbing of every impulse by turning to alcohol and drugs, while others seek instant material wealth by questionable investments or by dishonesty, with little or no regard for the consequences. Perhaps the practice of patience is more difficult, yet more necessary, now than at any previous time.

THE SCRIPTURES TEACH PATIENCE

To the Latter-day Saints, the Lord gave patience as one of the divine attributes that qualifies a person for the ministry (see D&C 4:6); He counseled them to be patient in their afflictions (see D&C 24:8; 31:9; 54:10; 98:23-24); and He admonished them to make their decisions in patience (see D&C 107:30). The Savior taught us to be perfect (see Matthew 5:48; 3 Nephi 12:48) and said, "Ye are not able to abide the presence of God now, neither the ministering of angels; wherefore, continue in patience until ye are perfected." (D&C 67:13.)

EXAMPLES OF PATIENCE

The Lord, Jesus Christ, is our perfect example of patience. Though absolutely unyielding in adherence to the truth, He exemplified patience repeatedly during His mortal ministry. He was patient with His disciples, including the Twelve, despite their lack of faith and their slowness to recognize and understand His divine mission. He was patient with the multitudes as they pressed about Him, with the woman taken in sin, with those who sought His healing power, and with little children. Finally, He remained patient through the sufferings of His mock trials and His crucifixion.

During the Apostle Paul's ministry of about thirty years, between his conversion and his martyrdom in Rome, he was flogged five times, beaten severely at least three times, imprisoned several times, shipwrecked three times, and stoned and left for dead on one occasion. (See 2 Corinthians 11:23-27.) Through all of this affliction, he continued his powerful ministry. He wrote to the Romans that God "will render to every man according to his deeds: To them who by patient continuance in well doing seek for glory and honour and immortality, eternal life: But unto them that are contentious [impatient], and do not obey the truth, but obey unrighteousness, indignation and wrath, Tribulation and anguish." (Romans 2:6-9.)

The Prophet Joseph Smith's afflictions and sufferings paralleled those of Paul in many respects. Beyond imprisonments, mobbings, and beatings, he suffered the anguish of betrayal by disloyal, unfaithful associates. But he offered the hand of friendship and fellowship to them even after they had opposed and betrayed him.

Some years ago, President Roy A. Welker of the German-Austrian Mission, one of the outstanding mission presidents of the Church, needed to assign a missionary to labor in Salzburg, Austria, to solve a problem in the branch there. Eight new missionaries were soon to arrive in the mission. He prayed that one of them would have the proper visa and currency to labor in Austria. He continued to pray and waited two weeks for an answer. The night before the eight arrived, the Spirit of the Lord whispered to the president the name of the missionary who should be assigned to Salzburg. The one whose name he received was the one who had the proper credentials to go to Austria. I was that elder.

The president's patience not only helped solve a problem in the branch, but it also blessed me and our family in a way that I never could have foreseen. Shortly after I arrived in Salzburg, that part of the German-Austrian Mission was changed into the Swiss-Austrian Mission. Later, I was transferred to Zurich, Switzerland, where I met Brother Julius Billeter, a warm and friendly member who was a genealogist. He was acquainted with the genealogical records of my progenitors. He researched the names of six thousand of my ancestors for whom temple work later was completed.

PATIENCE TODAY

We should learn to be patient with ourselves. Recognizing our strengths and our weaknesses, we should strive to use good judgment in all of our choices and decisions, make good use of every opportunity, and do our best in every task we undertake. We should not be unduly discouraged or in despair at any time when we are doing the best we can. Rather, we should be satisfied with our progress even though it may come slowly at times.

We should be patient in developing and strengthening our testimonies. Rather than expecting immediate or spectacular manifestations, though they will come when needed, we should pray for a testimony, study the scriptures, follow the counsel of our prophet and other Church leaders, and live the principles of the gospel. Our testimonies then will grow and mature naturally, perhaps imperceptibly at times, until they become driving forces in our lives.

Patience with family members and others who are close to us is vital for us to have happy homes. However, we often seem more willing to be courteous and polite with strangers than with those in our own family circles. For some reason, criticism, sharp language, and quarreling too often seem to be acceptable at home but not away from home.

Husbands, be patient with your wives; and wives, be patient with your husbands. Don't expect perfection. Find agreeable ways to work out the differences that arise. Remember President David O. McKay's wise counsel regarding marriage: Keep your eyes wide open before marriage and half closed afterward. (See Conference Report, April 1956, p. 9.) Perhaps, on occasion, our wives could get into the car and honk the horn while we, as husbands, get the children ready.

Parents, be patient with your children. Read to your little children and help them with their schoolwork, even if you need to tell or show them the same thing many times. Elder Richard L. Evans said, "If they find that they can trust us with their trivial questions, they may later trust us with more weighty ones." (Ensign, May 1971, p. 12.) Capitalize on their natural curiosity and help them develop a love for learning. Teach them the principles of the gospel in simple terms. Be patient with them if they disturb family home evening or family prayers. Convey to them the reverence you feel for the gospel, Church leaders, and the Savior.

Be patient with your youth, especially as they make the transition from adolescence to adulthood. Many of them have the appearance of adults and think they are adults, but they have had little experience with which to make adult judgments. Help them to get the experience they need and to avoid the pitfalls that can harm them.

On the other hand, I urge you children to be patient with your parents. If they seem to be out of touch on such vital issues as dating, clothing styles, modern music, and use of family cars, listen to them anyway. They have the experience that you lack. Very few, if any, of the challenges and temptations you face are new to them. If you think they know nothing about the vital issues I just mentioned, take a good look at their high school and college yearbooks. Most important, they love you and will do anything they can to help you be truly happy.

I advise you to be patient in financial matters. Avoid rash or hurried financial decisions; such decisions require patience and study. Get-rich-quick schemes seldom work. Beware of debt. Be especially careful of easily obtained credit, even if the interest is tax deductible. Young couples should not expect to begin their married lives with homes, automobiles, appliances, and conveniences comparable to those their parents have spent years accumulating.

Finally, a word about patience with our Heavenly Father and His plan of eternal progression. How incredibly foolish to be impatient with Him, the Father of our spirits, who knows everything and whose work and glory, through His Son, Jesus Christ, is "to bring to pass the immortality and eternal life of man." (Moses 1:39.) As Elder Neal A. Maxwell said, "Patience is tied very closely to faith in our Heavenly Father. Actually, when we are unduly impatient, we are suggesting that we know what is best — better than does God. Or, at least, we are asserting that our timetable is better than his. Either way we are questioning the reality of God's omniscience." (*Ensign,* October 1980, p. 28.)

Elder Richard L. Evans said, "There seems to be little

evidence that the Creator of the universe was ever in a hurry. Everywhere, on this bounteous and beautiful earth, and to the farthest reaches of the firmament, there is evidence of patient purpose and planning and working and waiting." (In Conference Report, October 1952, p. 95.)

Quoting from Elder Marvin J. Ashton: "We do not have to worry about the patience of God, because he is the personification of patience, no matter where we have been, what we have done, or what we, to this moment, have allowed ourselves to think of ourselves. . . .

"God will not forsake [us]." (*Speeches of the Year: BYU Devotional Addresses, 1972-73*, Provo, Utah: Brigham Young University Press, 1973, p. 104.)

I am truly grateful for the Lord's patience with His children. I am infinitely grateful for His patience with me and for the privilege I have to serve as a special witness of the divinity of Jesus Christ.

I am gratified, as I travel among the members of the Church, to see how many truly live the gospel principles. To them, I quote a promise given by the Lord: "Those that live shall inherit the earth, and those that die shall rest from all their labors . . . ; and they shall receive a crown in the mansions of my Father, which I have prepared for them.

"Yea, blessed are they . . . who have obeyed my gospel; for they shall receive for their reward the good things of the earth. . . .

"And they shall also be crowned with blessings from above." (D&C 59:2-4.)

Let us be patient, especially in adversity, as we meet our challenges of uncertainty, trials, pressure, and tribulation in today's world.

TO THE LONELY AND MISUNDERSTOOD

ELDER RICHARD G. SCOTT

Each passing day I am aware that there are many youth of the Church who understand the teachings of the Savior and apply them faithfully and consistently in their lives. They continue to grow in strength and self-confidence, and they find that their obedience is rewarded with happiness, peace, and self-assurance.

I am also aware that there is a significant number of youth who are striving to identify a path that will bring them satisfaction—a sense of belonging and of self-worth. Some have an intellectual knowledge of gospel principles but have not incorporated them completely into their own lives. They live partially or superficially the teachings of the Savior, and as a consequence, do not receive the fullness of direction that can come from the Lord or the ability to achieve blessings that result from being fully, willingly obedient to His commandments. They have not yet discovered the power and inspiration that come from the Lord to aid all of us in the difficult experiences of life. Such individuals strive mightily to face each day's challenges on their own, and they encounter difficulties. It is because I know that they see only a part of the picture, and can be stealthily led by Satan down erroneous paths, that I share some per-

161

sonal experiences that a kind and loving Lord has used to help me understand the meaning and power of some of the principles of His gospel.

I too have had such feelings of loneliness and of being left out and not appreciated.

I was born into a home where my father was not a member of the Church, and my mother was what some would categorize as inactive. During my early childhood, I didn't understand the significance of the fact that there was no priesthood-bearing patriarch or consistent teaching of gospel principles in our home. Yet no son could have been more proud of his father or loved him more than I did. He taught me and my brothers the importance of industry, integrity, education, manual skills, trust, and obedience. We gained self-confidence through the practice of these worthy traits. Because he traveled frequently and left our mother alone for significant periods of time to raise five active, exuberant boys, we discovered in her a marvelous combination of love, patience, firmness, and diligence. She was and continues to be more a friend and companion than anything else. (The Lord has since greatly blessed our family. Dad became a sealer in the Washington Temple, and mother serves with him as a temple worker. Both are powerful examples of righteous obedience.)

During my youth, understanding bishops and patient home teachers and other interested members encouraged us five boys to attend church and to participate in its activities. We did so, although at times reluctantly. I remember the times when I slipped out the back door as Sunday School began. There were, however, times when I listened to the teachings in class. I'm sure that if anyone had questioned my testimony and understanding of the gospel, I would have fiercely defended it as being strong and vigorous. Only with the perspective of time and many subsequent experiences of more active participation in the Church do I now realize that I knew very, very little of the true meaning of the gospel plan. I participated in church activities but somehow felt I was always at the periphery. I approached youth activities daydreaming of a glorious evening dancing with the most popular girls in the ward. The reality of each evening was quite different. As I sat on the sidelines and watched others enjoying themselves, I felt somehow left out, not part of the central group. The same occurred in school. Though I felt comfortable in academic activities, the social and sport activities left me feeling alone and unwanted. It wasn't until a lot later in life that I realized it was largely my fault.

I have since learned that one cannot demand love and respect or require that the bonds of friendship and appreciation be extended as an unearned right. These blessings must be earned. They come from personal merit. Sincere concern for others, selfless service, and worthy example qualify one for such respect. All my rationalization that others had formed select groups and knowingly ruled out my participation was largely a figment of my imagination. Had I practiced correct principles, I need not have felt alone.

Well did President McKay observe, "Every man, every person radiates what he or she is — every person is a recipient of radiation." ("The Times Call for Courageous Youth and True Manhood," Improvement Era, June 1969, p. 116.) Where proper gospel principles are observed, that radiation invites friendship and trust. Where they are lacking, there is a negative unpleasant radiation that closes the doors to righteous companionship.

During my last year at the university, I looked forward to a fine professional future and had my life very well outlined. Then a kind and thoughtful Lord placed a bombshell in my little world. Her name was Jeanene Watkins. Her father's call to the Senate had brought her to Washington, D.C., where I lived. The more I got to know her, the more fascinated I became; and each opportunity to be with her deepened the growing love within my heart. One evening as we conversed about the important things of life, she innocently said, "When I marry, I'll marry a returned missionary in the temple." That comment struck me to the core. It began a process of reflection, contemplation, and prayer that resulted in my receiving a call as a missionary to Uruguay.

I thought myself ill-prepared to teach the gospel to anyone. I had an intellectual understanding of some of the gospel principles that I recognized needed to be converted into a heart-centered, Holy Ghost-inspired, burning testimony of truth. I struggled to communicate to the Lord my feelings of gratitude for the privilege of service, for the blessing of righteous parents, and for the love of one of His most precious handmaidens. I asked Him to help me become an effective servant in His hands. I strained to forget self, struggled to help others, and in the process the skeleton of the teachings I had received took on new life and meaning.

I discovered that we are not left alone to face the challenges of life. We can receive guidance and strength from a loving, understanding God in heaven. I bathed my pillow with tears as I pled for the mercy of the Lord to forgive a wayward soul or to fortify a family in need. I pled that a heart could be softened or a struggling father could be given a personal witness of truth. And I discovered the limitless breadth of love.

Familiar scriptures through prayer and application guided new depths of understanding and appreciation. I had read the words many times. They now took on new meaning: "And charity suffereth long, and is kind, and envieth not, and is not puffed up, seeketh not her own, is not easily provoked, thinketh no evil, and rejoiceth not in iniquity but rejoiceth in the truth, beareth all things, believeth all things, hopeth all things, endureth all things.

"Wherefore, my beloved brethren, if ye have not charity, ye are nothing, for charity never faileth. Wherefore, cleave unto charity, which is the greatest of all. . . .

"But charity is the pure love of Christ, and it endureth forever; and whoso is found possessed of it at the last day, it shall be well with him." (Moroni 7:45-47.)

What a priceless message for any that would enjoy the comforting circle of true friendship! How I wanted to share those exquisite feelings of love and appreciation—for belonging.

There were then, as now, constantly new lessons. Well do I remember the first time when, as I pled with the Lord for the help and guidance and feeling of support I had come to cherish, there was no answer. Instead I felt a barrier—an insurmountable wall. I reviewed my life, my feelings, my acts—anything that could affect such communication—and found no problems. It was not until after more purposeful struggling that there came the clarification. What I had felt was not a wall but a giant step—an opportunity to rise to a higher spiritual plane, an opportunity evidencing trust that I would obey correct principles without the necessity of constant reinforcement. After more effort, the peaceful comforting presence of the Spirit returned.

I wish I had some magic wand that would allow me to reach beyond the pages and touch the hearts of each to whom this message is intended and communicate the experiences that have flowed from a loving Father since that time, but I cannot. I can, however, mention four principles I have come to recognize as the foundation of happiness and growth and the secure feeling of companionship with the Lord.

These four principles have brought the deepest feelings of worthwhileness, peace, and happiness into my own life. The Lord has established these cornerstones in His eternal plan, and each one is essential. All work together in harmony to reinforce one another; and when they are applied with diligence and consistency, they produce strength of character and increasing ability to convert the challenges of life into stepping-stones to happiness now and forever. They are: first, faith in the Lord Jesus Christ and His teachings; second, repentance to rectify the consequences of mistakes of omission or commission; third, obedience to the commandments of the Lord to provide strength and direction in our lives; and fourth, selfless service to enrich our daily existence.

Satan also knows that these principles, if observed consistently, will render an individual increasingly resistant to his temptations. He has developed a comprehensive plan to undermine or destroy each one of them. For example, to dispose of faith Satan would plant and cultivate in each one of us the seeds of selfishness. He knows that if left unchecked, these seeds will grow into a monster that can consume and destroy the divine spirit in man. Selfishness is at the root of sin. It reinforces destructive habits that produce a dependence on chemical or physical stimulants that destroy the mind and body. Selfishness leads to unrighteous acts that debauch and deprave the soul.

Satan's program is based on immediate gratification of selfish desires — participate now and pay later. Yet the full terrible consequences of payment are never revealed until it is tragically late.

The spirit of the Lord can overpower the stifling effort of selfishness. That spirit comes with faith, repentance, obedience, and service.

With the other Brethren, I have the privilege of interviewing youth who have stumbled along the way and yet have painstakingly found their way back. Many are anxious to serve a mission. Their backgrounds vary widely, as does the degree of their transgression. The support from others ranges from strong to nonexistent. Yet there is always a common thread of similarity. In every case, without exception, each has come to the realization that wickedness never was happiness. Each has resolved to place into effect the saving principles of the gospel. The proper use of free agency produces the miracle of rebuilt, useful lives.

I have personally verified that until words such as *faith*, *prayer*, *love*, and *humility* become a living part of us through personal experience and the sweet prompting of the Holy Spirit, they hold no great significance and produce no miracles. I found that I could learn gospel teachings intellectually and through the power of reason and analysis recognize that they were of significant value. But their enormous power and strength and ability to stretch me beyond the limits of my imagination did not become reality until patient, consistent practice allowed the Holy Spirit to distill and expand their meaning in my heart.

The genius of the gospel plan is that by doing, principally in selfless service to others, those things the Lord counsels us to do, we are given every understanding, every capacity, every capability necessary to provide rich fulfillment in this life and the preparation necessary for eternal happiness in the presence of the Lord.

Yet anyone who paints a picture of life as being easy, without challenge, is either not being honest or has not yet encountered the growing experiences the Lord gives His children to prepare them for happiness in this life and the blessing of dwelling eternally in His presence.

The purpose of these experiences has been clarified by the Lord: "And if men come unto me I will show unto them their weakness. I give unto men weakness that they may be humble; and my grace is sufficient for all men that humble themselves before me; for if they humble themselves before me, and have faith in me, then will I make weak things become strong unto them." (Ether 12:27.)

Elder Orson F. Whitney wrote: "No pain that we suffer, no trial that we experience is wasted. It ministers to our education, to the development of such qualities as patience, faith, fortitude and humility. All that we suffer and all that we endure, especially when we endure it patiently, builds up our characters, purifies our hearts, expands our souls and makes us more tender and charitable, more worthy to be called the children of God . . . and it is through sorrow and suffering, toil and tribulation, that we gain the education that we come here to acquire and which will make us more like our Father and Mother in heaven." (As quoted in *Faith Precedes the Miracle*, p. 98.)

We can, however, avoid unnecessary sorrow and distress. President N. Eldon Tanner has wisely counseled: "The first thing to remember is that if we really understand and live the principles of the gospel, we won't find ourselves in some of the predicaments we get into. Much of the loneliness, heartache and despair which is common to so many people have come because either they or someone in their family or their mate did not live the principles of the gospel, or did not apply the principle of repentance.

"That is the second thing to remember. If you do get into trouble, or have not kept the commandments and have transgressed, then we have this glorious principle of repentance to help us erase the guilt and start all over again. The Doctrine and Covenants tells us, 'By this ye may know if a man repenteth of his sins—behold, he will confess them and forsake them.' (D&C 58:43.)"

Some of us divert our best efforts from constructive

accomplishment by investing them in mental anguish and continual worry. The Lord has taught me a great lesson about worry that I would like to share with you today. After a wonderful full-time mission, where everything that has subsequently proven to be of eternal value in my life began to mature, I was sealed in the temple to my lovely Jeanene. She had fulfilled her mission while I was serving mine. We began our life together with every expectation of happiness, having some understanding of the application of the principles of the gospel in our lives. I was blessed, I'm convinced, through the kindness of the Lord to obtain a job in a new, highly developmental pioneer effort to place a nuclear plant in a submarine. The work was fascinating, challenging, and absorbing. When combined with the natural growth experiences that come with the formation of a new family unit and Church assignments, I found each day fully occupied.

Within eight months, I was in the office of a doctor being carefully examined to determine if I had ulcers. For weeks I returned home from work each night with a severe headache. Only after a long quiet period of isolation could I calm my nerves sufficiently to sleep briefly and return to work the next day. I began to prayerfully consider my plight. It was ridiculous. All I wanted to do was be a worthy husband and father and carry out honorably my Church and professional assignments. But my best efforts produced frustration, worry, and illness. In time, I was prompted to divide mentally and physically, where possible, all of the challenges and tasks and assignments given to me into two categories: First, those which I had some ability to control and resolve I put into a mental basket called "concern." Second, all the rest of the things that were either brought to me or I imagined I had the responsibility to carry out but had no control over, I put in a basket called "worry." These were

169

things I could not change to any significant degree, so I studiously strived to completely forget them. The items in the "concern" basket were ordered in priority. I conscientiously tried to resolve them to the best of my ability. I realized that I could not always fulfill all of them on schedule or to the degree of competence I desired, but I did my best.

Occasionally as I sat in my office, I'd feel my stomach muscles tighten and tension overcome me. At that point I would cease whatever activity I was engaged in and, with earnest prayer for support, concentrate on relaxing and overcoming the barrier that worry produced in my life. Over a period of time, I came to understand how the Lord is willing to strengthen, fortify, guide, and direct every phase of life. The symptoms of illness passed, and I learned to face tasks under pressure.

Why is there such emphasis in the world today on things? When things become an end unto themselves — the object of our effort rather than tools to be used to reach greater and more noble goals — they become part of Satan's plan to deflect us from the Lord's program. They can lead us carefully down to hell. Things do not produce happiness on earth, and they don't provide exaltation. Material things are to be respected for their value as tools. Every artist, surgeon, or writer needs tools. They become instruments for greater good and should not at any time be the ultimate goal of life.

Many of life's disappointments come from looking beyond the mark, from seeking success and happiness where it cannot be found. When wealth, position, influence, and power become measures of success in life, we should not be disappointed when their attainment does not produce the satisfaction and blessings promised for fulfillment of the commandments of the Lord.

The Savior declared as His work and glory "to bring to

170

pass the immortality and eternal life of man." (Moses 1:39.) He enthroned love for one another, service to neighbors, and building the kingdom of God for His glory and majesty as noble and worthy goals that produce rewards beyond all power of expression.

The prophet Mormon gave us precious insight when he declared: "For behold, the Spirit of Christ is given to every man, that he may know good from evil; wherefore, I show unto you the way to judge; for every thing which inviteth to do good, and to persuade to believe in Christ, is sent forth by the power and gift of Christ; wherefore ye may know with a perfect knowledge it is of God.

"But whatsoever thing persuadeth men to do evil, and believe not in Christ, and deny him, and serve not God, then ye may know with a perfect knowledge it is of the devil; for after this manner doth the devil work, for he persuadeth no man to do good, no, not one; neither do his angels; neither do they who subject themselves unto him." (Moroni 7:16-17.)

I have obtained a personal witness that the true monument to an individual is worthy accomplishment, not mounds of paper plans or hoards of accumulated possessions. The eternal progress we attain in our own life and contribute to accomplish in the lives of others are measure enough for the worthwhileness of our efforts here on earth. No matter who we are, what lofty position we hold, or powerful influence we wield, these things in and of themselves are of no lasting moment. Rather, how well we serve as instruments in the hands of the Lord to accomplish His divine will, or how devotedly we obey His commandments and worthily we receive His ordinances — these things *are* important. In the final analysis, all success can be measured by how effectively we interpret and accomplish the will of our Father in Heaven in our own lives, the lives of our family and loved ones, and the lives of His other children we are blessed to serve.

Once in my life I had the feelings of being left out. I now share the companionship of incomparable brotherhood and sisterhood, a feeling of belonging, of being useful. And I recognize that it comes only from sincere striving to live the commandments of the Lord.

There are those about us on every side who feel rejected and who would justify taking a path contrary to that of the Lord. How essential it is to touch such a heart and have it feel the expanding influence of the Holy Ghost, to show to such an individual how every problem of life can be corrected when the gospel is allowed to flow into one's life!

BE THE BEST OF
WHATEVER YOU ARE

ELDER L. TOM PERRY

One of the most inspiring sermons I have had the privilege of hearing was delivered about the time I entered high school in one of our assemblies. This sermon was delivered by a member of our stake presidency. He was the owner and operator of the local hardware store, a man who was familiar with hand tools, so it was natural for him to talk about the most common tool of all—the hammer.

He told the story of a French carpenter in the early 1800s who had difficulty keeping his productivity high because the head on the hammer kept coming off as he worked. He spent half of his time chasing the flying hammerhead. He tried everything to keep the head on. He tried to nail it on. He soaked it in water. He even tried to glue it. Each process helped only for a short time before the hammerhead was again separated from the handle.

All of the carpenters in the country had the same problem, and all had resigned themselves to living with the situation—all except this man. He desired to be the best carpenter in all of France, and he reasoned that the only way he could become the best was to build a better hammer. Each evening after working hours, he thought about what could be done to develop a better hammer. Finally, after years of work, he discovered a new concept. It was a simple solution, but it worked. He made the bottom of the hammerhead smaller than the top and then drove a wedge into the top of the hammer. As long as the wedge was in place, the hammerhead could not come off. In fact, the more pressure applied to the hammerhead, the more pressure there was on the wedge to keep it in place. He had built the world's greatest hammer — one that has become the pattern for most all hammers even to this day. His was not the world's greatest discovery, but in his own field this carpenter became the best.

> If you can't be a pine on the top of the hill,
> Be a scrub in the valley — but be
> The best little scrub by the side of the rill;
> Be a bush if you can't be a tree.
> If you can't be a highway then just be a trail,
> If you can't be the sun be a star;
> It isn't by size that you win or you fail —
> Be the best of whatever you are!

(Douglas Malloch, "Be the Best of Whatever You Are," as cited in *The Best Loved Poems of the American People*, Garden City, New York: Doubleday, 1936, pp. 102-3.)

I will discuss three areas where I would like to challenge you to be the best with the great potential our Father in Heaven has blessed you with.

First, we are all children of our Heavenly Father. One of the greatest weaknesses in most of us is our lack of faith in ourselves. One of our common failings is to depreciate our tremendous worth.

A firm I was associated with some time ago embarked on a great executive development program at considerable expense. The program was open to all who expressed an interest. All an employee had to do was sign up. The firm paid the costs and even allowed employees one hour off from their normal daily work for classroom time—a free opportunity for an education in the art of management. During the two years the program was offered, only 3 percent of the employees signed up for the course. I have observed another situation where this 3 percent statistic seems to be somewhat reliable as the number of the divine children of our Father in Heaven who have enough faith in themselves to make the effort to do something important with their lives. Surely we could never be numbered among the 97 percent who are not taking advantage of opportunities. The scriptures tell us of our divine nature. Do you remember what the Psalmist said?

"O Lord our Lord, how excellent is thy name in all the earth! who hast set thy glory above the heavens. . . .

"When I consider thy heavens, the work of thy fingers, the moon and the stars, which thou hast ordained;

"What is man, that thou art mindful of him? and the son of man, that thou visitest him?

"For thou hast made him a little lower than the angels, and hast crowned him with glory and honour." (Psalm 8:1, 3-5.)

Have you ever thought of yourself as being a "junior angel"? Brigham Young has further defined our eternal relationship:

> Things were first created spiritually; the Father actually begat the spirits, and they were brought forth and lived with him. . . .
>
> I want to tell you, each and every one of you, that you are well acquainted with God our Heavenly Father. . . . You are all well acquainted with him, for there is not a soul of you but what has lived in his house and dwelt with him year after year; and yet you are seeking to become acquainted with him, when the fact is, you have merely forgotten what you did know.

There is not a person here today but what is a son or a daughter of that Being. In the spirit world their spirits were first begotten and brought forth, and they lived there with their parents for ages before they came here. . . .

We are the sons and daughters of celestial Beings, and the germ of the Deity dwells within us. . . .

We are all his children. We are his sons and daughters naturally, and by the principles of eternal life. We are brethren and sisters. (*Discourses of Brigham Young,* comp. John A. Widtsoe, Salt Lake City: Deseret Book Co., 1973, pp. 50, 53.)

History has abundantly given evidence of man's potential when he allows himself to be led by the power of the Lord. Do you remember the story of Joseph who was sold into Egypt? He was sent by his father to check on the welfare of his brothers as they tended the flocks. When they saw him coming, they satisfied the jealousy in their hearts and sold him for twenty pieces of silver to merchants on their way to Egypt. In Egypt, Joseph was purchased by Potiphar, the captain of the guard. Even as a servant in a far-off land, as a slave to a foreigner, he soon distinguished himself. The scriptures record:

"And the Lord was with Joseph, and he was a prosperous man; and he was in the house of his master the Egyptian.

"And his master saw that the Lord was with him, and that the Lord made all that he did to prosper in his hand.

"And Joseph found grace in his sight, and he served him: and he made him overseer over his house, and all that he had he put into his hand." (Genesis 39:2-4.)

Joseph's life continued to have its ups and downs. He found himself accused falsely of being unfaithful to his master and was cast into prison. Once again, because of his faithfulness, the Lord provided an opportunity for him to interpret Pharaoh's dream. Joseph was given the opportunity because of this interpretation to serve Pharaoh. He so distinguished himself in this service that he became a ruler in

Egypt while being only thirty years of age. Listen to the honor that Pharaoh bestowed upon him:

"And Pharaoh said unto his servants, Can we find such a one as this is, a man in whom the spirit of God is?

"And Pharaoh said unto Joseph, Forasmuch as God hath shewed thee all this, there is none so discreet and wise as thou art:

"Thou shalt be over my house, and according unto thy word shall all my people be ruled: only in the throne will I be greater than thou.

"And Pharaoh said unto Joseph, See, I have set thee over all the land of Egypt.

"And Pharaoh took off his ring from his hand, and put it upon Joseph's hand, and arrayed him in vestures of fine linen, and put a gold chain about his neck;

"And he made him to ride in the second chariot which he had; and they cried before him, Bow the knee: and he made him ruler over all the land of Egypt." (Genesis 41:38-43.)

Note the characteristic which distinguished Joseph to both Potiphar and the Pharaoh: "a man in whom the spirit of God is."

We each have the choice of being worldly like unto the brothers of Joseph or living worthy of the blessings of the Lord like unto Joseph. President Marion G. Romney said: "We mortals are in very deed the literal off-spring of God. If man understood, believed and accepted this truth and lived by it, our sick and dying society would be reformed and redeemed and men would have peace and eternal joy." With this divine knowledge burning within our souls, surely much will be expected of us. As a child of God, be the best of whatever you are.

The second challenge pertains to service in God's kingdom here upon the earth. One of the most exciting blessings which can come to us as members of our Savior's church is to live in this modern day when the Church is experiencing its greatest period of growth. Each day since the restoration of the gospel there has been greater opportunity for service in the Church than there was the day before. Tomorrow there will be an even greater opportunity than there is today. Certainly, this is the day spoken of by the ancient prophet when he said:

"And it shall come to pass in the last days, that the mountain of the Lord's house shall be established in the top of the mountains, and shall be exalted above the hills; and all nations shall flow unto it.

"And many people shall go and say, Come ye, and let us go up to the mountain of the Lord, to the house of the God of Jacob; and he will teach us of his ways, and we will walk in his paths." (Isaiah 2:2-3.)

As I travel throughout the stakes of the Church there is always one common cry: "If I only had another bishop like Brother Jones or another Relief Society president like Sister Smith or another Young Adult representative like Sister Brown or another home teacher like Brother Doe, what a difference I could make in my stake." I wonder if one reason hundreds of thousands more are not embracing the gospel is that we have not yet developed a strong enough leadership base. Do you see what a great demand there is for qualified leaders in our Father in Heaven's kingdom?

"For Zion must increase in beauty, and in holiness; her borders must be enlarged; her stakes must be strengthened; yea, verily I say unto you, Zion must arise and put on her beautiful garments." (D&C 82:14.)

Some labor with the misconception that their professions are too demanding to allow for a life of major service in the kingdom of God. My experience has been that the greatest teacher is service in His kingdom.

When I was a young man in my late twenties, and after just six months' experience in the retail business, I was offered the position of controller in a small store in central Idaho. I had about a month in this new position before I could acquire a place of residence for my family to come and join me. During that month, I almost lived at the store. A twenty-four-hour workday was a common occurrence as I attempted to keep pace with the responsibility I had been given.

One evening just after my family arrived, a car pulled up in front of our home and I was invited to come out and visit with a member of our stake presidency and a member of our ward bishopric. I was shocked with the announcement that a change was being made in our bishopric and I had been selected to be the second counselor. My first reaction was to say, "No, I am too busy." But the training of my parents rang louder than my first reaction, and I agreed to serve. This first experience in the bishopric was the best education I have ever received in organization and management. I found the Lord's way was transferable to business. As I practiced in business the techniques taught to me in Church service, I became more efficient in my business assignments. I soon found myself with more time for family, Church, and business responsibilities. The second great benefit was the experience of the joy of service in the Church. Next to my family, the most rewarding experiences in my life have been Church service opportunities.

This is the most exciting era the Church has ever known. Don't deprive yourself of a most rewarding opportunity of being prepared and willing to serve the Master. As a servant in His kingdom, be the best of whatever you are.

The final area I would like to discuss is our obligation to the earth and the nation in which we live. I recall a trip I made to one of the great nations of the world. We were so impressed with the people. How friendly and considerate they were to us! I told my wife, "If you want to have fun in this country, go out and get lost. Those people are so great at giving directions when you ask for assistance. They tell you where to go with such detail and then repeat it two or three times to be certain you understand."

This country was, however, in one of its most difficult periods. After suffering during World War II, the people went into a great rebuilding program. As things became easy again, they started to relax and wanted only to enjoy life. Their great interest became the pub and the television. If an industry was in difficulty, rather than attempting to solve the problem, it was much easier and more secure to turn it over to the government and nationalize it. One by one, the government found itself operating more and more businesses. To offset this great national power, the workers banded together and acquired so much control that they could paralyze the nation anytime it was to their advantage to call a strike.

A strike was in progress while we were there. Public buildings were completely without heat. Television stations were required to close down at 10:30 P.M. Stores were only allowed to turn on their lights one half of each working day. Shopping in stores during the period without lights was interesting. There would be one light burning at the entrance to the store. As you would step into the selling departments to shop, a salesperson would carry lanterns around to show you the merchandise. In one store, the temperature was 45 degrees. The saleslady explained they had been without heat all winter. The work week was reduced to three days. In hotels, you would find each room equipped with a candle and a note stating the lights could be turned out at any time. The heat was on in the hotel only during the evening and early morning hours. Having a haircut was an experience. The barbershop was cold and dark. The barber seated you in a chair and then ran downstairs to turn on a little handmade generator operated by his former Honda. One neon tube then came on and the barber commenced to cut your hair. I was greatly relieved to go outside after the haircut and find that my ears were still in place. On top of all this, the people had to live with the realization that if the strike continued two additional weeks, all power would be turned off.

The economic pressures caused the government to fall, and a general election was called. This election was held while we were there. Unfortunately, the election just highlighted problems rather than solved them. There had been such lack of interest for so long that the elections failed to turn up new leadership. The vote was split between the two major parties. One received the popular-vote margin. The second received the greater number of seats in the governing body. Neither had the majority to rule. A small third party was now in control and could bargain for the best deal. The ability to organize the government rested in its hands. Radical leaders could demand positions of importance and power in the new government far beyond what they were entitled to as representatives of the people.

This is a classic example, to me, of what occurs when complacency and the desire for security supersede the desire for freedom and the willingness to sacrifice for its preservation. I wish that this were an isolated case of the problems of just one nation. Unfortunately, the cry is being heard from almost all free nations for willing, dedicated, honest leadership to guide their countries through troubled times.

I challenge you as a citizen to be the best of whatever you are.

We currently find ourselves in a situation where we have experienced a period of unprecedented prosperity that has caused us to become soft and spoiled. We have again reached the point where we demand much more than we are willing to give. We have become self-centered and worldly. We turn to things of man rather than to things of God.

We know the ultimate outcome of such a course. We know the suffering, bloodshed, sorrow, and despair which will follow if this direction is not changed. The immediate question that comes to mind when we examine our current state of affairs is, Why must we be knocked to our knees before we start on the road to recovery? The answer is obvious: The cycle can be reversed at any point. All that is needed is inspired leadership to give direction.

Where can we expect to find that leadership today? In the book of Ether a great truth is given: "In the gift of his Son hath God prepared a more excellent way." (Ether 12:11.) We have been promised, "And if your eye be single to my glory, your whole bodies shall be filled with light, and there shall be no darkness in you; and that body which is filled with light comprehendeth all things." (D&C 88:67.) The only missing ingredient to make our contribution as leaders in God's kingdom is found in the Doctrine and Covenants: "If ye have desires to serve God ye are called to the work; For behold the field is white already to harvest." (D&C 4:3-4.)

There has never been a time in the history of the world when those who are prepared to give honest, inspired leadership have greater opportunity than there is today. Isn't this the time for those who have been given the knowledge of the truth, the light of the gospel, to stop testing the line between right and wrong and enthusiastically embark on that which the Lord has asked us to do? Isn't this the time in our preparation to do all we have been assigned, and then just a little bit more? Isn't this the time in our nation to fill our responsibilities as good citizens, and then just a little bit more?

I know by personal experience that the more you serve the Lord, the greater are His blessings to you. There is no greater joy than being a builder in His kingdom. I challenge you with all of the great power and potential that is within you to be the best of whatever you are.

THE PRICE OF PEACE

PRESIDENT MARION G. ROMNEY

I have chosen the subject the price of peace because of the world's overwhelming concern for peace — and our clear failure to obtain it. Sadly, in our search for peace, we seem, as Paul so aptly said, "Ever learning, and never able to come to the knowledge of the truth." (2 Timothy 3:7.) We also seem, as Isaiah said, in "a dream of a night vision . . . as when an hungry man dreameth, and, behold, he eateth; but he awaketh, and his soul is empty." (Isaiah 29:7.)

When I was in the military service during the First World War, we were told that we were "making the world safe for democracy"; we were fighting a war to end all wars. When my eldest son was in the military during the Second World War, he was told that he was preserving the cause of liberty and freedom. The same rationale has continued for the past several decades.

Why is it that our generation, with all its vaunted learning, has failed so miserably in its pursuit of peace? The only answer I can give you is that we are not willing to pay the price for it. My purpose here is to point out that price.

Peace has been variously defined, but perhaps we might think of it as "harmony within one's self, and with God and man." This conception includes all elements in the dictionary definition.

The condition opposite to peace and harmony, say the lexicographers, is characterized by conflict, contention, disputation, strife, and war.

Let us consider these two descriptions of peace and its antithesis in light of scripture. Let me first note, however, that I lay my case upon the scriptures, believing, as I do, that they contain the revealed word of God and that God, knowing all things, has spoken ultimate truth. Now to the scripture:

"The works of the flesh," says the Apostle Paul, include "adultery, . . . lasciviousness, idolatry, . . . hatred, variance, . . . wrath, strife, . . . envyings, murders, drunkenness, . . . and such like." (Galatians 5:19-21.) Note how closely these works of the flesh resemble conflict, contention, disputations, strife, and war — the antithesis of peace and harmony.

"But the fruit of the Spirit," continues Paul, "is love, joy, peace, longsuffering, gentleness, goodness, faith, meekness, temperance" (Galatians 5:22-23) — the very elements of the peace we seek.

From these descriptions, is it not clear that what we have to do to get peace is obtain the fruit of the Spirit? Or to put it another way, because Lucifer "is the father of contention" (3 Nephi 11:29), the antithesis of peace, the price of peace is victory over Satan.

I know that there are some in the world who deny the existence of a personal Satan. This denial is false, being sponsored by the father of lies himself, but there is nothing new about it. The anti-Christs, at his bidding, have denied the existence of Satan from ancient times. The fact is, however, that Lucifer is a personage of spirit, just the same as Jesus and you and I were personages of spirit before we

185

were born. In the spirit world, he was a personage of great ability. Isaiah refers to him as a son of the morning. "O Lucifer, son of the morning! how art thou cut down to the ground," he laments. (Isaiah 14:12.)

Yet Lucifer rejected the Father's plan for the salvation of the human race and sought to substitute his own plan. Not prevailing, he, with one-third of the hosts of heaven, was "cast down, and . . . became Satan . . . the father of all lies, to deceive and to blind men, and to lead them captive at his will," that is, those who will "not hearken unto my voice." (Moses 4:3-4.)

One of Satan's dupes, by the name of Korihor, having been stricken dumb because he repeatedly denied the existence of God, "put forth his hand and wrote, . . . I know that I am dumb, for I cannot speak; and I know that nothing save it were the power of God could bring this upon me; yea, and I always knew that there was a God.

"But behold, the devil hath deceived me; for he appeared unto me in the form of an angel, and said unto me: Go and reclaim this people, for they have all gone astray after an unknown God. And he said unto me: There is no God; yea, and he taught me that which I should say. And I have taught his words; and I taught them because they were pleasing unto the carnal mind; and I taught them, even until I had much success; insomuch that I verily believed that they were true; and for this cause I withstood the truth, even until I have brought this great curse upon me." (Alma 30:52-53.)

You see, Korihor knew, right while he was denying their existence, that there was a Satan and that there was a God. Many of Korihor's modern counterparts fulfill the prediction of Nephi, who, speaking of our times, said:

"At that day shall he [the devil] rage in the hearts of

the children of men, and stir them up to anger against that which is good.

"And others will he pacify, and lull them away into carnal security, that they will say: All is well in Zion, yea, Zion prospereth, all is well—and thus the devil cheateth their souls, and leadeth them away carefully down to hell.

"And behold, others he flattereth away, and telleth them there is no hell; and he saith unto them: I am no devil, for there is none—and thus he whispereth in their ears, until he grasps them with his awful chains, from whence there is no deliverance." (2 Nephi 28:20-22.)

Now, we may rest assured of this: If there is no devil, there is no God. But there is a God and there is a devil, and the bringing of peace requires the elimination of Satan's influence. Where he is, peace can never be. Further, peaceful coexistence with him is impossible. He cannot be brought to cooperate in the maintenance of peace and harmony. He promotes nothing but the works of the flesh.

"Whatsoever thing persuadeth men to do evil, and believe not in Christ, and deny him, and serve not God, then ye may know with a perfect knowledge it is of the devil; for after this manner doth the devil work, for he persuadeth no man to do good, no, not one; neither do his angels; neither do they who subject themselves unto him." (Moroni 7:17.)

As a prelude to peace, then, the influence of Satan must be completely subjugated. Even in heaven there could be no peace with him after his rebellion. There, in the world of spirits, the Father and the Son could find no ground upon which they could cooperate with him. He had to be cast out—not compromised with, but cast out.

"No man," said Jesus, "can serve two masters: for either he will hate the one, and love the other; or he will hold to the one, and despise the other. Ye cannot serve God and mammon." (Matthew 6:24.)

Earth life is a period of trial for every person of two mighty forces pulling in opposite directions. On the one hand is the power of Christ and His righteousness. On the other hand is Satan and his fellow travelers. Mankind, in the exercise of their God-given moral agency, must determine to travel in company with the one or the other. The reward for following the one is the fruit of the Spirit — peace. The reward for following the other is the works of the flesh — the antithesis of peace.

For six thousand years the campaign for the souls of men has been waged by Satan with unabated fury. The widespread debauchery, idolatry, contention, bloodshed, suffering, and sorrow under which the inhabitants of the earth have groaned through the centuries testify to the fact that Satan has always wielded a potent influence.

But while, as a general rule, the works of the flesh have flourished, there have been at least two periods of peace — and there will be another yet to come.

The Nephites, following the ministry of Jesus among them, abolished the works of the flesh and obtained the fruit of the Spirit. This is the way they did it: "The disciples of Jesus had formed a church of Christ. . . . And as many as did come unto them, and did truly repent of their sins, were baptized in the name of Jesus; and they did also receive the Holy Ghost. And . . . in the thirty sixth year, the people were all converted unto the Lord." Consequently, "there were no contentions and disputations among them . . . because of the love of God which did dwell in [their] hearts. . . . There were no envyings, nor strifes, nor tumults, nor whoredoms, nor lyings, nor murders, nor any manner of lasciviousness; . . . but they were in one, the children of Christ, and heirs to the kingdom of God . . .

and every man did deal justly one with another. . . . And surely," says the record, "there could not be a happier people among all the people who had been created by the hand of God." (See 4 Nephi 1:1-2, 15-17.)

This condition prevailed among them for almost two centuries. Then, deserting the gospel of Jesus Christ, the Nephites turned to the works of the flesh, and "there began to be among them those who were lifted up in pride, . . . and they began to be divided into classes; and they began to build up churches unto themselves to get gain, and began to deny the true church of Christ." There were also among them some "churches which professed to know the Christ, and yet they did deny the more parts of his gospel," — a perfect prototype of our times. Now, these churches "did multiply exceedingly because of iniquity, and because of the power of Satan who did get hold upon their hearts." (4 Nephi 1:24-28.) Thus yielding to Satan, this Nephite people, which through strict obedience to the gospel of Christ had enjoyed perfect peace for nearly two centuries, was, within another two centuries, utterly destroyed as a nation in a civil war.

Another people who achieved peace were the people of Enoch who lived before the flood. They came to peace in the same manner as did the Nephites, and they enjoyed the same felicity. But they did not thereafter yield to Satan and return to the works of the flesh, as did the Nephites. On the contrary, they continued in their righteousness and "the Lord came and dwelt in righteousness." And they "built a city that was called the City of Holiness, even Zion," which in the "process of time, was taken up into heaven," where it now is. (Moses 7:16-21.)

Of all the descendants of Adam and Eve, these people of Enoch are the only ones, so far as I am informed, who have obtained lasting perfect peace.

189

As it was with the Nephites and the people of Enoch, so it has always been and always will be; for banishing Satan by living the gospel of Jesus Christ is the price of—and the only way to—peace. God, in His infinite solicitude for the welfare of His children, charted for them this way to peace in the beginning of the world, and He has recharted it in every dispensation since. He has just as consistently sounded warnings of disasters that follow abandonment of that course. If a single person, yielding to Satan, is filled with the works of the flesh, he wars within himself. If two yield, they each war within themselves and fight with each other. If many people yield, a society flourishes with the harvest of great stress and contention. If the rulers of a country yield, there is worldwide contention, for as the prophet Isaiah says, "The wicked are like the troubled sea, when it cannot rest, whose waters cast up mire and dirt. There is no peace, saith my God, to the wicked." (Isaiah 57:20-21.)

As the works of the flesh have universal application, so likewise does the gospel of peace. If one man lives it, he has peace within himself. If two men live it, they each have peace within themselves and with each other. If the citizens live it, the nation has domestic peace. When there are enough nations enjoying the fruit of the Spirit to control world affairs, then, and only then, will the war drums throb no longer, and the battle flags be furled in the Parliament of Man, the Federation of the World. (See Alfred, Lord Tennyson, "Locksley Hall," *The Complete Poetical Works of Tennyson,* ed. W.J. Rolfe, Boston: Houghton-Mifflin Co., 1898, p. 93, lines 27-28.)

Now there are individuals who try to serve the Lord without offending the devil. They raise in the minds of many truth seekers the vexing question, Is there not some middle ground upon which peace may be secured and maintained? Must the choice lie irrevocably between peace on the one hand, obtained by compliance with the gospel of Jesus Christ, and contention and war on the other hand?

In answer to this question, I feel safe in saying that if there is a middle ground it is as yet undiscovered; and that, too, notwithstanding the fact that the search for it has been long and tortuous. Ignorant of, or ignoring, and without any thought of paying the price of peace, men have tried many approaches. There was St. Pierre's project in 1713; Bentham's plan, 1780; Kant's project, 1795. There were the Hague Conferences of 1899 and 1907, and the League of Nations following World War I, to name but a few. There have been pacts, treaties, and alliances, *ad infinitum,* all without success.

Sometimes we put great well-meaning hope — even desperate hope — in the works and wisdom of man. I remember that just before the First World War broke out in August 1914, Dr. David Starr Jordan, then honorary chancellor of Stanford University, and an eminent advocate of peace, stated that the conditions of the world made any great war between the nations impossible, that there never would be another great international war, that the world had passed beyond that stage of savagery.

Said Elder James E. Talmage, who heard him speak, "He showed that the business interests were so closely knit that if a nation should be so rash as to declare war upon another, the bankers would veto the declaration because they had too much at stake; and that if the voice of the bankers was not heeded then the people would rise up and say, 'There shall be no war.' . . . Then by another splendid array of facts he showed the prospective cost of warfare in this day and proved to his own satisfaction that there was not wealth enough in the world to keep up a big war for more than a very few months. When he had closed his address, [Elder Talmage said] to him: 'I wish I could believe

191

you, doctor.' 'You do not believe me?' 'I do not.' 'And why?' 'Because you have left out some of the most important factors of your problem.' 'And what are they?' 'The words of the prophets; and in a matter that concerns the existence of nations I shall consider the words of the prophets in preference to the deductions of the academician, even though he be as distinguished as yourself, sir.' " (James E. Talmage, *Liahona*, 5:677-79.)

The fact that within the thirty years following Dr. Jordan's prediction the world passed through two World Wars and has since had three decades of wars and rumors of wars brings to mind the words of the Lord through the mouth of Isaiah: "The wisdom of their wise men shall perish, and the understanding of their prudent men shall be hid." (Isaiah 29:14.)

If we would have peace, we must make up our minds to pay the price of peace. Such is the word of God, and such is the verdict of six thousand years of human history.

Now, while I feel that many people of the earth today are so infected with the works of the flesh that they do not recognize them as such, and, therefore, many people are not possessed of the moral courage to pay the price of peace, still we should not, Jonah-like, sulk under a vine if some of them should turn to apply the principles of the Prince of Peace and find its joyful rewards. On the contrary, we should rejoice, for to proclaim peace is the sole purpose of our life's mission. We should find no pleasure in the fact that men's strivings for peace have proved ineffectual. I wage no war against their efforts. Many of them are doing the best they can in the light they have. Nevertheless, I can see no justification for us, who have the clear light of the revealed gospel of Christ, to spend our lives stumbling around through the mists following the uncertain glimmer of a flickering candle lighted by the wisdom of men. Rather, we should devote our energies to spreading the true light, and leave the mists to those who do not see that light.

Yet, even as we try to teach the gospel of peace, we see that most people would prefer to focus on other aspects of the problem. Even so, we should not live a life of despair and gloom. We should enjoy life in the light of revealed truth and keep ourselves advised as to what the Lord has said about the price of peace.

I am grateful that the days of my probation have come in this dispensation, in which the light of revealed truth shines in all its effulgent glory. I know of no other time in which I would have preferred to live. If in the providence of God, holocausts come, the earth will not disintegrate or be rendered uninhabitable, neither will all the peoples of the earth be destroyed. It will be part of the prophets' road to the dawn of a glorious millennium of perfect peace. For this I know—and of it you may likewise be assured—in the end, righteousness will triumph; the powers of darkness will be put to flight; peace will come.

Let us as a people vow to apply in our individual lives, in our homes, in our businesses, in all our relationships with others and each other the principles of the restored gospel of Jesus Christ. The fruit of its spirit brings and establishes peace. And each of us may have peace in ourselves if we are willing to pay the price.

The Peaceable Things
of the Kingdom

ELDER DEAN L. LARSEN

In a revelation to Joseph Smith, the Lord gave this simple description of the plan of life and salvation: "And this is my gospel — repentance and baptism by water, and then cometh the baptism of fire and the Holy Ghost, . . . which showeth all things, and teacheth the peaceable things of the kingdom." (D&C 39:6.)

It is apparent from this statement that those who follow the principles of the gospel should be able to experience the "peaceable things." Yet in this stressful period in which we live, we frequently encounter people who seem to be doing the best they know how to avoid the evils of the world, who desire very much to be good, but who suffer from unhappiness, frustration, and confusion. It is one of the paradoxes of our time.

I would like to offer some thoughts and suggestions about how we might better enjoy the "peaceable things of the kingdom" and free ourselves from the despondency and hopelessness that sometimes seem to beset so many.

All of us feel the urgency to perfect ourselves — to learn, to grow, to achieve, to produce. Some of these pressures can be constructive and helpful if they are not allowed to become overwhelming, especially if they are generated by our own initiative.

LEARN PATIENCE

One of the first important lessons of survival in this stressful time is to learn patience. Perfection is not achieved in one spasmodic burst of effort. As we move along the path of progress, we must find moments of enjoyment and refreshment along the way.

Orin L. Crain had this need in mind when he penned the following lines:

Slow me down, Lord!
Ease the pounding of my heart
By the quieting of my mind.
Steady my hurried pace
With a vision of eternal reach of time.
Give me,
Amidst the confusion of my day,
The calmness of the everlasting hills.
Break the tensions of my nerves
With the soothing music of the singing streams
That live in my memory.
Help me to know
The magical restoring power of sleep.
Teach me the art
Of taking minute vacations of slowing down
    to look at a flower;
    to chat with an old friend or make a new one;
    to pet a stray dog;
    to watch a spider build a web;
    to smile at a child;
    or to read a few lines from a good book.
Remind me each day
That the race is not always to the swift;
That there is more to life than increasing its speed.
Let me look upward

Into the branches of the towering oak
And know that it grew great and strong
Because it grew slowly and well.
Slow me down, Lord,
And inspire me to send my roots deep
Into the soil of life's enduring values
That I may grow toward the stars
Of my greater destiny.
(Reprinted in the *Ogden Standard Examiner* by Abigail
Van Buren.)

Such interludes as Mr. Crain recommends help us to recognize the "peaceable things" and to rejuvenate our energies and commitment for a renewed effort.

On one occasion Joseph Smith made the following declaration: "When you climb up a ladder, you must begin at the bottom, and ascend step by step, until you arrive at the top; and so it is with the principles of the Gospel—you must begin with the first, and go on until you learn all the principles of exaltation. But it will be a great while after you have passed through the veil before you will have learned them. It is not all to be comprehended in this world; it will be a great work to learn our salvation and exaltation even beyond the grave." (*Teachings of the Prophet Joseph Smith*, p. 348.)

Jacob's citation of the Zenos allegory in the Book of Mormon makes much the same expression: "Ye shall clear away the branches which bring forth bitter fruit, according to the strength of the good and the size thereof; . . . Wherefore ye shall clear away the bad according as the good shall grow, . . . until the good shall overcome the bad." (Jacob 5:65-66.)

Some of us create such a complexity of expectations for ourselves that it is difficult to cope with the magnitude of them. Sometimes we establish so many particulars by which to evaluate and rate ourselves that it becomes difficult to feel successful and worthy to any degree at any time. We can drive ourselves unmercifully toward perfection on such a broad plane. When this compulsion is intensified by sources outside ourselves, the problem is compounded. Confronting these demands can bring mental and emotional despair.

Everyone needs to feel successful and worthy in some ways at least part of the time. The recognition of our frailties need not propel us to try to achieve perfection in one dramatic commitment of effort. The best progress sometimes comes when we are not under intense duress. Overzealousness is at least as much to be feared as apathy. Trying to measure up to too many particular expectations without some sense of self-tolerance can cause spiritual and emotional burnout.

In order to avoid the effects of too many external and internal pressures, it is not necessary or wise to withdraw from all of life's challenges. This would only compound our difficulties. To enjoy the "peaceable things of the kingdom," we must find warm acceptance, love, and understanding from those who have the most direct influence on our lives.

It is helpful to remember the Savior's parable of "counting the cost" (Luke 14:28) before we launch into any enterprise. When we simultaneously branch out into too many channels, we may not have the strength or the resources to sustain the effort, and frustration will result.

Having patience requires that we maintain a proper balance in our lives. Bryant S. Hinckley had this in mind when he said: "If we are over enthusiastic, our enthusiasm may become fanaticism. If we are strongly emotional, our emotion may lead to hysterics. If we are excessively imaginative, . . . we may become visionary and flighty. . . . If we have a superabundance of courage, it may manifest itself in recklessness. . . . If we are super-sympathetic, our sympathy can become a weakness and run into sentimentalism. If we are original, our originality may become an eccentricity. Piety may become sanctimoniousness. And so every virtue may become a vice — every grace a defect. It is the fine balance of these virtues that makes the strong man." (Bryant S. Hinckley, *A Study of the Character and Teachings of Jesus of Nazareth: A Course of Study for the Adult Members of the Aaronic Priesthood,* Salt Lake City: The Church of Jesus Christ of Latter-day Saints, 1950, pp. 169-70.)

It is important to discuss also the need for developing an appropriate degree of self-tolerance. While we cannot allow ourselves to become slothful and lackadaisical in our efforts toward self-improvement, we cannot afford to lose all sense of patience and charity toward ourselves when we occasionally come short of perfection.

We are more than mechanical units. Our personalities are in a process of becoming, they are growing — an inner flowering. This development does not occur in one day. We are like all others in some respects, but in some respects each of us is unique. There has never been anyone exactly like you. There never will be. Never will anyone possess your special individuality and your particular possibilities.

In light of these facts, one of the least profitable things we can do is to compare ourselves with others. Generally, when we make such comparisons, we match our weaknesses against the most prominent talents and virtues of those we admire or envy. No one comes out well in this useless game. Its effects can be devastating.

It is necessary to accept ourselves with a self-love that is neither vain nor selfish, but rather one that is tolerant and understanding, one that we might feel toward an old friend. Your friend may have his flaws. He has limitations, but over the years you have come to recognize his good qualities. Sometimes you simply put up with him when he is overbearing and foolish. But he is your friend.

Part of enduring to the end is related to our attitudes toward ourselves. When we have a high enough regard for ourselves, we can overcome setbacks and still go forward. It is difficult to defeat a person who is determined to endure in this sense.

Another quality we must have in order to enjoy the peaceable things of the kingdom is a trust in the ultimate triumph of good over evil. Sometimes much desired blessings for which we have worked hard to qualify seem to be long in coming. At other times the unfairness and arrogance of others appear to go unpunished. There are times when we cannot seem to see our way through a maze of difficulties and hard times to a satisfactory conclusion. These are some of the most severe tests of our mortal existence.

True religious faith helps us to establish such a trust. Experience ultimately teaches us that honest effort will finally be rewarded, and that wickedness, in the end, will not produce happiness. When we cannot see the end from the beginning as the Lord does, it is sometimes a challenge to trust in His promise. But experience will confirm the validity of the trust.

Lorenzo Snow, who knew something of challenge and disappointment in his own lifetime, once made this observation to the Saints who were weighed down by the severity of their circumstances: "How ill-qualified we were one year ago to pass through the scenes through which we have been led with success. From which let us realize the folly of an over-anxiety to pry into the scenes that are lying before us, inasmuch as God will prepare a way by a gradual process, step by step, and leading us forward in a manner that will prove easy as we pass along, but which, if presented to our view at once, would seem insurmountable."

There is the story of two neighboring farmers—one a habitual Sabbath-breaker, and the other a faithful observer of the Lord's day. On one occasion the Sabbath-observer severely chastised his neighbor for working his farm on Sundays rather than attending to his religious devotions. This led to an argument and a challenge. "Let us put the matter to a test," the Sabbath-breaker said. "We will select two pieces of ground of equal size and fertility. On them we will plant the same crop. My piece of ground I will work only on Sundays, and you will work yours on the other days of the week. Then we will see who gets the greater harvest."

The challenge was accepted and the conditions were faithfully observed. As the harvest was gathered in, the Sabbath-observing farmer was disappointed to learn that the piece of ground farmed by his neighbor had produced the greater yield. The Sabbath-breaker exulted in his apparent triumph and his discrediting of the contention of his faithful neighbor.

"You have forgotten one important thing," protested the Sabbath-observer. "The Lord doesn't always settle his accounts in October."

Related to this same matter of trust is the principle taught in the Savior's parable of the talents. An honorable effort, given to the full by the two honest servants, brought the same reward from the master even though the product of their efforts was not the same.

It has seemed to me that built into the conscience of every human soul is the most accurate determiner of whether we are living in such a way as to merit the ultimate blessings promised to the faithful. We point to this determiner when we say, "Be honest with yourself." A person does not easily deceive his own conscience. Deep within our own hearts we generally know when we have paid the price, when we have done the best our personal resources and abilities would have allowed us to do at the moment, regardless of the outcome of our effort or the way it may be viewed by others. It is at these times that we know real peace, even though the product of our effort may not be all that we would have hoped it to be. The full return on this kind of investment cannot always be determined at the next audit period.

When Jesus was crucified by His detractors, it appeared to all observers — even to His disciples — that His efforts had accounted for nothing. But the Savior knew He had paid the price. History has borne record to the quality of His investment.

Another factor that has a bearing upon whether or not we experience peace in our lives has to do with our being able to realistically respond to expectations that others have for us and the demands they sometimes make of us. In responding to these expectations, we must successfully evaluate between fundamentally important values and the sometimes superficial or outward performances that others may expect from us. This requires that we recognize real truth and demonstrate integrity to it. Peace of mind comes when we know we are doing the right things for the right reasons.

For some reason, one of the most common methods many of us use to motivate is to develop feelings of guilt within ourselves or in others for whom we have a responsibility. Guilt feelings are a natural product of an injured conscience. When we willfully violate a valid code of conduct, we suffer the consequences of our infraction in the internal conflict that occurs within our own souls. Such feelings, painful and remorseful though they may be, can generate the desire to repent and improve. They can be useful, constructive emotions that propel us forward to greater perfection.

But purposely generating feelings of guilt over some shortcoming as a means of motivating action or promoting more compliant behavior is rarely productive. The devastating effect of a child's constantly being told that he is stupid, lazy, or ugly has been well documented in behavioral studies. When anyone's honest effort to *do* better or to *be* better is met by debilitating criticism, real motivation and incentive are often destroyed. All of us profit from encouragement and from occasional constructive correction. But we must be helped to feel that we are valued and appreciated in spite of our shortcomings.

I have been appalled when I have heard leaders attempt to extort greater devotion and exertion from young missionaries by telling them they will never rise above the level of their performance on their missions. This is foolishness. I have lived long enough to see many contradictions to this contention. It is as though our performance in any given period of our lives rivets us forever to an inescapable course. If this were a true principle, repentance and reformation would be impossible.

My final suggestion for experiencing peaceable things probably has the best possibility for producing immediate results. It is a simple formula that will almost always work. Raise your own spirits by finding something to do that will lift others. Nothing seems to have a greater power for turning us away from our own self-pity and despondency than to focus upon something good we can do for someone else who has a need.

Erich Fromm has said: "The most important sphere of giving . . . is not that of material things, but lies in the specifically human realm. What does one person give to another? He gives of himself, of the most precious he has, he gives of his life. This does not necessarily mean that he sacrifices his life for the other—but that he gives him of that which is alive in him; he gives him of his joy, of his interest, of his understanding, of his knowledge, of his humor, of his sadness — of all expressions and manifestations of that which is alive in him. . . . He does not give in order to receive; giving is in itself exquisite joy. But in giving he cannot help bringing something to life in the other person, and this which is brought to life reflects back to him; in truly giving, he cannot help receiving that which is given back to him." (*The Art of Loving,* New York: Bantam Books, Inc., 1970, pp. 20-21.)

And Leona Fetzer Wintch adds this: "A famous man recently summed up his life's work by saying he had given so much away, he had only a little of himself left to die. He forgot that the bookkeeping of life's ledger shows that the more a man gives of his love and of himself, the more he has. There are no limits to which the soul can extend itself, and this boundless dominion is immeasurably increased by the very act of sharing." (*Life is Fissionable.*)

I am continually impressed by some instruction the Savior gave to His disciples near the close of His mortal ministry. It has the nature of being "bottom line" to all of His gospel teaching. You will be very familiar with this scripture, but consider it again carefully.

> When the Son of man shall come in his glory, and all the holy angels with him, then shall he sit upon the throne of his glory:
> And before him shall be gathered all nations: and he shall separate them one from another, as a shepherd divideth his sheep from the goats:
> And he shall set the sheep on his right hand, but the goats on the left.
> Then shall the King say unto them on his right hand, Come, ye blessed of my Father, inherit the kingdom prepared for you from the foundation of the world:
> For I was an hungred, and ye gave me meat: I was thirsty, and ye gave me drink: I was a stranger, and ye took me in:

Naked, and ye clothed me: I was sick, and ye visited me: I was in prison, and ye came unto me.

Then shall the righteous answer him, saying, Lord, when saw we thee an hungred, and fed thee? or thirsty, and gave thee drink?

When saw we thee a stranger, and took thee in? or naked, and clothed thee?

Or when saw we thee sick, or in prison, and came unto thee?

And the King shall answer and say unto them, Verily I say unto you, Inasmuch as ye have done it unto one of the least of these my brethren, ye have done it unto me.

Then shall he say also unto them on the left hand, Depart from me, ye cursed, into everlasting fire, prepared for the devil and his angels:

For I was an hungred, and ye gave me no meat: I was thirsty, and ye gave me no drink:

I was a stranger, and ye took me not in: naked, and ye clothed me not: sick, and in prison, and ye visited me not.

Then shall they also answer him, saying, Lord, when saw we thee an hungred, or athirst, or a stranger, or naked, or sick, or in prison, and did not minister unto thee?

Then shall he answer them, saying, Verily I say unto you, Inasmuch as ye did it not to one of the least of these, ye did it not to me.

And these shall go away into everlasting punishment: but the righteous into life eternal. (Matthew 25:31-46.)

I think there is nothing we can do to develop godlike qualities that is more important than giving of ourselves in the way described here by the Savior. It seems to make the ultimate difference with Him when it comes to the time of judgment. And I believe it has some of the highest prospects for helping us overcome any unhappiness we may be experiencing ourselves.

It would not be appropriate if I did not mention personal prayer and regular study of the scriptures as having a great influence in lifting us from feelings of frustration or despondency.

As we pass through the challenges, the setbacks, and the occasional disappointments that all of us experience, may we gain reassurance from the recognition that achieving perfection is a long-term endeavor and that we can trust in the fact that right will prevail. And may we have the charity toward ourselves and others that will allow us to enjoy regularly the "peaceable things" of the kingdom.

THANKS BE TO GOD

ELDER NEAL A. MAXWELL

The Lord has described His plan of redemption as the Plan of Happiness. (See Alma 42:8, 16.) Indeed, it is, but none of us is likely to be a stranger to sorrow.

Conversationally, we reference this great design almost too casually at times; we even sketch its rude outlines on chalkboards and paper as if it were the floor plan for an addition to one's house. However, when we really take time to ponder the Plan, it is breathtaking and overpowering! Indeed, I, for one, cannot decide which creates in me the most awe—its very vastness or its intricate, individualized detail.

The vastness of it all is truly overwhelming. We are living on a small planet which is part of a very modest solar system, which, in turn, is located at the outer edge of the awesome Milky Way galaxy. If we were sufficiently distant from the stunning Milky Way, it would be seen as but another bright dot among countless other bright dots in space, all of which could cause us to conclude, comparatively, "that man is nothing." (Moses 1:10.)

Yet we are rescued by such reassuring realities as that God knows and loves each of us—personally and perfectly. Hence, there is incredible intimacy in the vastness of it all.

Are not the very hairs of one's head numbered? Is not the fall of each sparrow noticed? (See Matthew 10:29-30.) Has Jesus not borne, and therefore knows, our sins, sicknesses, and infirmities? (See Alma 7:11-12.)

Furthermore, the eventual purpose of it all is centered not on some other cosmic concern but on us — "to bring to pass the immortality and eternal life of man." (Moses 1:39.) President Brigham Young said there are millions of earths like this one so that certain planets, as Isaiah said, are formed to be inhabited (see Isaiah 45:18) as God's plan of salvation is executed and reexecuted. How glorious is our God! Truly, as the Psalmist said, "We are the people of his pasture, and the sheep of his hand." (Psalm 95:7.)

Has He not even told us that His "course is one eternal round"? (D&C 3:2.) Are we not also given intriguing intimations such as how "planets . . . move in their times and seasons" and how "all these kingdoms, and the inhabitants thereof" are to know the joy of seeing the countenance of the Lord — "every kingdom in its hour, and in its time, and in its season"? (See D&C 88:42, 43, 61.)

In fact, has not the Almighty Father, who oversees it all, shared with us almost more than we can comprehend about His work? But we can understand enough to trust God regarding that which we do not understand.

Even so, since God is so serious about our joy, can we safely postpone striving to become like Him? Since there can be no true joy for us apart from doing His work, can we risk being diverted by other chores? Dare we stop short of enduring "well to the end"? Can we not be thankful for a purposeful life even when we have a seemingly purposeless day? Should we not be grateful for God's plan for us even when certain of our own plans for ourselves go awry?

Of course, this grand plan and design for our happiness is not something that exists merely to strike awe in us or to evoke gasps of gladness. It does not exist apart from us either, but completely involves us — painfully at times and happily at other times — but relentlessly always.

This plan is underscored by a deep, divine determination, and "there is nothing that the Lord thy God shall take in his heart to do but what he will do it." (Abraham 3:17.) Once the plan became operational (and it was with our enthusiastic consent, by the way), it could not be altered just because you and I (in the midst of an otherwise good life) might have a difficult day or a soul-stretching season in our lives. Such were clearly foreseen by Him, and long ago we were deemed, if obedient, adequate to meet all such challenges. Yes, we will often feel inadequate, but fortunately He knows us far better than we know ourselves.

Let us, therefore, feast upon a few of the gospel truths that pertain to our Father's Plan of Happiness.

The implications for this, our second estate, are many, once we realize this life is (1) a divinely designated proving ground (see Abraham 3:25); (2) a circumstance in which those who triumph overcome by faith that is deliberately tried (D&C 76:53); and (3) an unusual environment featuring, among other things, a dimension called time. (See Alma 40:8.)

It seems clear (not only scripturally but logically) that this second estate could not include either the direct memories or the reference experiences of our first estate. If such were to impinge overmuch upon this second estate, our mortality would not be a true proving ground.

In like manner, the veil also stands between us and that which lies ahead, our third and everlasting estate. If, for instance, our association with resurrected beings in this second estate were the order of the day, if they walked with us in the marketplace and conversed with us in the Gospel

Doctrine class, no true growth or test, as were envisioned, could really occur.

Therefore, much as we might like to have the curtains parted so that (not only "on a clear day" but all the time) we could see forever, thereby knowing the circumstances, events, and challenges which lie ahead of us — those things are, for the most part, kept carefully from us. Indeed, it appears that such understanding is usually given only to those individuals who have progressed sufficiently spiritually, that they can be trusted with such knowledge, because it will not distract or divert them or cause them to slacken.

To give people spiritual knowledge — in advance of their capacity to understand it or to apply it — is no favor. (See Matthew 7:6.) Even yesterday's righteous experience does not guarantee us against tomorrow's relapse. A few who have had supernal spiritual experiences have later fallen. Hence, enduring well to the end assumes real significance, and we are at risk till the end!

Thus, the Lord has created this planet — our customized schoolhouse — so carefully in order that it would be environmentally inhabitable. Likewise, God has carefully designed the curriculum to be used therein to be strictly consistent with his proving purposes. Walter Bagehot put it well:

"If the universe were to be incessantly expressive and incessantly communicative, morality would be impossible: we should live under the unceasing pressure of a supernatural interference, which would give us selfish motives for doing everything, which would menace us with supernatural punishment if we left anything undone; we should be living in a chastising machine . . . the life which we lead and were meant to lead would be impossible . . . true virtue would become impossible . . . a sun that shines and a rain which falls equally on the evil and on the good, are essential to

morality in a being free like man and created as man was."
(*The Works of Walter Bagehot*, Hartford, Connecticut, ed.
Forrest Morgan, The Travelers Insurance Company, 1889,
2:313.)

Thus, while there is a spiritual ecology (and when we
violate it we pay a certain price), the costs or consequences
are not always immediate or externally visible.

Thieves are not always brought immediately to justice.
A child-abusing parent is not at once restrained. So, in a
hundred ways that could be illustrated, the outward judgment of God does not immediately fall upon an erring
individual so that this second estate may be a true proving
ground; and also, mercifully, so we can, if we will, know
the refreshment and renewal of repentance. Without repentance the past would forever hold the future hostage.

This mortal condition affords to all but those who die
young (but who die unto the Lord) options to choose among,
time enough to choose, and the opportunity to experience
the consequences of our choices — "according to the flesh."
(Alma 7:12.) So it is that most mortals live and learn (or
fail to learn) "in process of time." (Moses 7:21, 68.)

Since, for example, "almost all" individuals have a tendency to abuse power and authority — not just a few, not
even a mere majority — how are the relevant lessons about
the righteous use of power to be learned except in this
laboratory-of-life setting? Could we have truly experienced
the risks and opportunities of power merely by attending
some pointed lectures or doing some directed reading during
our first estate? Was it not necessary to experience, "according to the flesh," what it is like to be on the receiving
end of unrighteous dominion? And the necessity of repentance when one has been on the giving end? The general
absence, for instance, on the human political scene of attributes such as genuine humility, mercy, and meekness is

a grim reminder, again and again, of how essential these qualities are to the governance of self or a nation. (See D&C 121:34-44.)

In some respects, it is easier to govern a whole people than oneself. Of one ancient political leader it is candidly recorded: "And he did do justice unto the people, but not unto himself because of his many whoredoms; wherefore he was cut off from the presence of the Lord." (Ether 10:11.) One can cater to mortal constituencies but lose the support of the one Elector who matters!

We know that God's "word of power" brings entire new worlds into being and causes others to pass away. (See Moses 1:35-38.) But the powers of heaven cannot be handled or controlled except upon the basis of righteousness. (See D&C 121:36.) Real righteousness, therefore, cannot be a superficial, ritualistic thing. It must arise out of the deepest convictions of the soul, not out of a desire merely to "go along" with the Heavenly Regime simply because that's how things are done! God's power — unlike mortal power — is accessed only by those who have developed, to a requisite degree, God's attributes.

Jesus counseled us, too, concerning materialism and "the deceitfulness of riches" (Matthew 13:22), and of how hard it is for those who trust in riches and materialism to enter into the kingdom of God. (See Luke 18:24.) Another of those scalding but divine generalizations! The relevant mortal experiences permit (but do not guarantee) that we will learn about what should come first in life. Can those who are diverted by riches or the search for riches and thus fail to discern the real purposes of life be safely trusted with greater dominions which call for even greater discernment? "And he that overcometh, and keepeth my works unto the end, to him will I give power over the nations." (Revelation 2:26.)

Could we truly appreciate the supremacy of spiritual things without experiencing the limitations of material things? Not in just one brief encounter, but day by day?

Since "he that hath no rule over his own spirit is like a city that is broken down, and without walls" (Proverbs 25:28) — how could we learn to govern ourselves without the specific opportunities for growth and failure which daily life affords? In fact, is not managing life's *little* challenges so often the *big* challenge? Those who wait for a single, spectacular, final exam are apt to flunk the daily quizzes.

We are to strive to become perfect, even as our Father in Heaven is perfect. (See Matthew 5:48.) But this is not just generalized goodness; rather, it is the attainment of specific attributes.

So it is that, if God intends to use us (and He does), He must school us so that we emulate His attributes and function in harmony with the laws of His universe while yet in this "proving ground." We do not fully know why our obedience in the *here and now* is so crucial, but it is no doubt bound up in our *usefulness* and *happiness* in the *there and then*.

Moreover, even when we fail to develop an eternal attribute sufficiently, our mortal experiences will nevertheless have shown us just how precious that attribute is. How much easier, later on, to accept with appreciation the righteous dominion of those who have so progressed. Again, could such appreciation and acceptance have been generated in the abstract?

We are even reassured that our mortal performance will be judged according to what has been allotted to us and how we use our talents within that allocation. (See Alma 29:3, 6; Matthew 25:14-30.) We will not be able to invoke, justifiably, either deprivational or circumstantial evidence in our own behalf later on to show that we were dealt with unjustly. The record will be clear! Perhaps that stark reality will contribute to the response of those who, at judgment time, will wish to be buried under mountains and rocks to hide them from the face of God! (See Revelation 6:16.)

Thus, the whole mortal schooling process has been so carefully structured to achieve results that could be achieved in "no other way." (Helaman 5:9.) We can come to know the Lord as our loving, tutoring Father and God—but not as a policeman posted at every intersection of our lives.

Hence, our submissiveness to the Lord must be the real thing, not the equivalent of obeying the speed limit only as long as the highway patrolman is there in his pace car. Indeed, awaiting full development is our willingness "to submit to all things which the Lord seeth fit to inflict upon [us], even as a child doth submit to his father." (Mosiah 3:19.) This is a sobering gospel truth about submissiveness. It is a wintry declaration. This truth is not likely to evoke from us an "Oh, goodie" response!

During our schooling in submissiveness, we will see the visible crosses some carry, but other crosses will go unseen. A few individuals may appear to have no trial at all, which, if it were so, would be a trial in itself. Indeed, if our souls had rings, as do trees, to measure the years of greatest personal growth, the wide rings would likely reflect the years of greatest moisture—but from tears, not rainfall.

Most of our suffering comes from sin and stupidity; it is, nevertheless, very real, and growth can occur with real repentance. But the highest source of suffering appears to be reserved for the innocent who undergo divine tutorial training.

Thus we see how gospel truths concerning the plan of salvation are much more than a "tourist guide" for the second estate; they include a degree of understanding of what Paul called "the deep things of God." (1 Corinthians

2:10.) In our moments of deep anguish, suffering, and be-wilderment — in those moments when we ask in faith for certain outcomes and are refused, because to give them to us would not be "right" (3 Nephi 18:20) — then our faith is either deepened or slackened.

Yes, even in our prayers, we can, unintentionally, ask "amiss." (2 Nephi 4:35.) No wonder humility is such an everlasting virtue. For us to accept God's "No" as an affirma-tive indication of his love — rather than a lack thereof — and as a signal that we have asked amiss, this is true humility.

How often have you and I in our provincialism prayed to see ahead and, mercifully, been refused, lest our view of the present be blurred?

How many times have we been blessed by *not* having our prayers answered, at least according to the specifications set forth in our petitions?

How many times have frustrating, even gruelling, ex-periences from which we have sought relief turned out, later on, to have been part of a necessary preparation that led to much more happiness?

"And now when Alma heard this . . . he beheld that their afflictions had truly humbled them, and that they were *in a preparation to hear the word.*" (Alma 32:6; italics added.)

How many times have we impatiently expressed our discontent with seemingly ordinary and routine circum-stances that were divinely designed, shaping circumstances for which, later on, we were very grateful? Alas, have there perhaps not also been those times when we have been grumpy with God or, unlike Job, even "charged God fool-ishly"? (Job 1:22.) How many times, naively, have we vig-orously protested while on our way to a blessing?

Therefore, our faith in and thanksgiving for Heavenly Father, so far as this mortal experience is concerned, consists not simply of a faith and gladness that He exists but also

214

includes faith and thanksgiving for His tutoring of us to aid our acquisition of needed attributes and experiences while we are in mortality. We trust not only the Designer but also His design of life itself—including our portion thereof.

Our response to the realities of the plan should not be resignation or shoulder-shrugging fatalism—but reverential acceptance. If, at times, we wonder, we will also know what it is to be filled with wonderment.

Why should it surprise us, by the way, that life's most demanding tests as well as life's most significant opportunities for growth in life usually occur within marriage and the family? How can revolving-door relationships, by contrast, be a real test of our capacity to love? Is being courteous, one time, to the stranger on the bus as difficult as being courteous to a family member who is competing for the bathroom morning after morning? Does fleeting disappointment with a fellow office worker compare to the betrayal of a spouse? Does a raise in pay even approach the lift we receive from rich family life?

Besides, even the most seemingly ordinary life contains more than enough clinical opportunities for our personal growth and development. By the way, while mortality features "an opposition in all things" (2 Nephi 2:11), we need feel no obligation to supply opposition or to make life difficult. Sufficient unto each situation are the challenges thereof.

Should it surprise us that in striving to acquire and develop celestial attributes, the greater the interpersonal proximity the greater the challenge? Is not patience, for instance, best developed among those with whom we interface incessantly? The same is true with any of the other eternal attributes. Hence the high adventure of marriage and family life—and why it is that so many run away from these challenges, thinking they can avoid having to confront themselves by losing themselves in other endeavors or life-styles.

Is not gospel perspective about the plan of salvation so precious, therefore, in the midst of "all these things" which are designed to give us experience?

Yes, let us be filled with an attitude of thanksgiving in our journey homeward, but not become too comfortable here, as C.S. Lewis observed: "Our Father [in Heaven] refreshes us on the journey [through life] with some pleasant inns, but [he] will not encourage us to mistake them for home." (C.S. Lewis, *The Problem of Pain,* New York: Macmillan, 1967, p. 103.)

Nor should the praise and positions accorded to us by men in the second estate come to matter too much either, as an aging but articulate Malcolm Muggeridge observed of his own mortal journey:

"Now, the prospect of death overshadows all others. I am like a man on a sea voyage nearing his destination. When I embarked I worried about having a cabin with a porthole, whether I should be asked to sit at the captain's table, who were the more attractive and important passengers. All such considerations become pointless when I shall soon be disembarking." (*Things Past,* ed. Ian Hunter, New York: William Morrow and Company, Inc., 1979, p. 166.)

And when the gossamer veil called time is "too much with us," let us recall that, ere long, time will be no more. Time is measured only to man anyway. (See Revelation 10:6; Alma 40:8; D&C 84:100.) Meanwhile, let us make allowance for the rapidity with which time seems to pass, especially when we are happy. Jacob found it so: "And Jacob served seven years for Rachel; and they seemed unto him but a few days, for the love he had to her." (Genesis 29:20.) On such a scale each of us has but a few days left in mortality.

As men or women of Christ, we can be led by Him

through this second estate, in the words of Helaman, "in a straight and narrow course across that everlasting gulf of misery which is prepared to engulf the wicked—

"And land their souls, yea, their immortal souls, at the right hand of God in the kingdom of heaven, to sit down with Abraham, and Isaac, and with Jacob, and with all our holy fathers, to go no more out." (Helaman 3:29-30.)

"*To go no more out.*" An intriguing promise! For the busy, for those ceaselessly on the move, for the homeless, for the lonely, and for widows and widowers—and for others of us who will become such—does not the prospect of this homecoming in such grand and everlasting circumstances warm the soul? Not, of course, that life hereafter is to consist of unending repose. Rather, for those who attain the presence of God, "to go no more out"—nowhere is really out of His presence, and now is forever! As time is no more, likewise space will shrink irrevocably. For all we know, the speed of light may prove to be too slow to do some of what must be done.

No wonder it is called the Plan of Happiness! No wonder the divine and prophetic exhortations to us are so straightforward and repetitive! No wonder we should be so thankful, so everlastingly thankful! Is God's Plan of Happiness not a most fundamental cause for thanksgiving this day and always?

INDEX